2 CORINTHIANS
A SELF-STUDY GUIDE

Irving L. Jensen

MOODY PRESS
CHICAGO

Contents

Introduction

A study of Paul's two letters to the Corinthians is a study of obstacles encountered in the proclamation of the gospel. Happily, more is written in the epistles about *solutions* than about the problems themselves. In 1 Corinthians the problems are mainly those of a local church. In the second epistle the same church in involved, but most of the discussion is about Paul's own dilemma, that of convincing his Corinthian brethren that he was a true apostle of Christ, preaching the true gospel of God. Among other things, your study of 2 Corinthians will give you a deeper appreciation of Paul the man and a more firm conviction of the truth and power of the gospel he preached.

Suggestions for Study

Here are suggestions for making your study of 2 Corinthians most effective:

1. Approach each lesson with the desire to learn what God has for you in the Bible text. Begin each study in prayer and ask the Holy Spirit to be your teacher.

2. Spend most of your time in the Bible text itself. This study guide continually directs you to the Scriptures. Be sure to read all references outside of 2 Corinthians as well.

3. Train your eyes to *see* what the Bible says. Look, look, look! is the urgent advice here.

4. Use *context* as your best aid in arriving at the meaning of the text. This is the reason for the lessons' constant reminder to look for *relationships*—for example, how one paragraph is related to another, and one verse to another verse.

5. Follow the "golden rule of interpretation" in your Bible study:

When the plain sense of Scripture makes common sense, seek no other sense; therefore, take every word at its primary, ordinary, usual, literal meaning unless the facts of the immediate context, studied in the light of related passages and axiomatic and fundamental truths, indicate clearly otherwise.

6. Use pencil or pen continually in your study. This cannot be overemphasized. Record observations, including answers to the questions of the manual, and the completion of analytical charts. Among other things, the work sheets for analytical charts encourage you to look for relationships, mentioned above.

7. Mark paragraph divisions clearly in your Bible before you begin your analysis of each passage. This is important.

8. If you are using the King James Version as your basic study text, refer to at least one or two contemporary versions for comparative purposes. Such aids are helpful for unclear passages. All Bible quotes in this study guide are from the King James Version unless otherwise stated.

9. Refer to commentaries only after you have completed your analysis of a particular part of the passage. The *Notes* section at the end of each lesson gives information concerning a Scripture passage that is not afforded by the text itself.

10. Study carefully the charts of each lesson. These will help you *see* more things in the passage being analyzed.

Suggestions to Group Leaders

1. *Length of study units.* There are thirteen lessons in this manual, but it is advisable to break up some lessons into smaller units because of their length. You as leader of the class should decide in advance how much of the lesson should be studied as homework.

2. *Homework.* Urge each member of the class to complete the analysis suggestions of the manual before coming to class. It is important that each member think and study for himself, so that he can weigh more accurately what someone else says about a Bible text. Encourage the class to bring questions about the text to the class hour for discussions.

3. *Class participation.* Encourage all members to participate orally in the class but don't put pressure in this direction. Also, never embarrass a person by underestimating the significance of an answer he gives or a question he might ask. Concerning his answer, he often has in mind *more* than he can put in words. Concerning questions, it is a healthy sign of mental activity when ques-

tions are asked, regardless of the kind. It is true that Bible teaching comes alive in an environment of asking questions.

4. *The class hour.* Here are practical hints:

(a) Open the class session on time with a brief, heartfelt prayer.

(b) Keep the entire meeting informal. It is not intended to be a formal worship service.

(c) The opening minutes should be devoted to welcoming visitors, reviewing the previous lesson, and identifying the goals of the present discussion.

(d) Devote most of the hour to free, informal discussion of the main parts of the lesson. Illustrate the Bible passages from your own experience and encourage the members of the class to do the same.

(e) As you approach the end of the meeting, summarize the things learned and let the members suggest ways to apply the Bible truths.

(f) Make clear what the homework is for the next meeting.

(g) Close the meeting on time. Any further discussion, if sought by members, should be kept distinct from the stated class meeting hour.

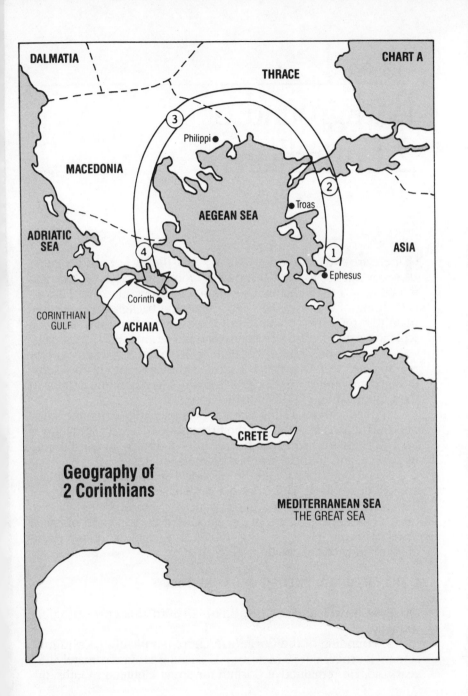

DALMATIA

CHART A

THRACE

MACEDONIA

③ Philippi ●

② ● Troas

AEGEAN SEA

ADRIATIC SEA

① ● Ephesus

ASIA

④ ● Corinth

CORINTHIAN GULF

ACHAIA

CRETE

Geography of 2 Corinthians

MEDITERRANEAN SEA
THE GREAT SEA

Lesson 1
Background of 2 Corinthians

There are two main sources for studying the background of Paul's second letter to the Corinthians. One is the book of Acts, and the other is 1 Corinthians. The summary below titled The Historical Setting of 2 Corinthians represents the background supplied mainly by those two books. Study this summary carefully, and you will have a good grasp of what caused the writing of 2 Corinthians.

It would be helpful to begin your study of background by reading Acts 18:1-18*a*. This is Luke's historical record of Paul's *first* evangelistic ministry in Corinth. You will learn here the origins of the gospel witness in this notable Greek city.

It goes without saying that the best preparation for the study of 2 Corinthians is a study of the first epistle.[1] The self-study guide on 1 Corinthians furnishes descriptions of the city of Corinth and its people, and so these will not be repeated here.

Some questions about the historical setting of 2 Corinthians are still unresolved. This does not jeopardize a profitable study of the epistle, however. For a book of such an intensely personal nature, 2 Corinthians excels in the amount of doctrine and practical Christian living it teaches. This will become evident in the course of your study of the epistle itself.

I. THE HISTORICAL SETTING OF 2 CORINTHIANS

Observe how 1 and 2 Corinthians fit into this chronological sequence:

1. Founding of the Corinthian church, on Paul's second missionary journey, A.D. 50 (Acts 19:1-17). Paul was approximately fifty years old. He remained at Corinth for about eighteen months, liv-

---

1. Not all title combinations in the Bible (e.g., 1, 2, 3 John) have such detailed historical connections as do Paul's two epistles to the Corinthians.

ing with Aquila and Priscilla and working part time in the tent-making business to support his evangelistic ministry.
2. Arrival at Ephesus on the third missionary journey, A.D. 52. Paul had these two contacts with the Corinthian church before writing 1 Corinthians from Ephesus:
(a) A short visit to combat incipient opposition to the apostle's ministry, and to correct other evils.[2] His mission was apparently not effective. (Read 2 Cor. 2:1; 12:14; 13:1-2. Note the reference to a forthcoming "third time" visit.)
(b) A letter referred to in 1 Corinthians 5:9. At least part of this so-called "previous letter' was written to correct existing evils in the church. The letter is not part of the New Testament canon, because it was not divinely inspired Scripture.[3]
3. A three-year teaching and evangelistic ministry in Ephesus on this third missionary journey (Acts 19:8, 10; 20:31; 1 Cor. 16:8), including a fruitful ministry (Acts 19:10-12, 17-20) and severe trials (Acts 19:9; 19:21–20:1; 20:31; 2 Cor. 1:8). Paul writes 1 Corinthians toward the end of this mission, around A.D. 55. Titus may have been the one to deliver the letter to Corinth. (If the short visit mentioned above was not *before* writing 1 Corinthians, it would be placed here.)
4. A "painful" letter to the church (2 Cor. 2:3-4; 7:8).[4] This may have concerned an offense given to Paul in person during the short visit cited above. (Cf. 2 Cor. 2:5-11.) Titus may have been the bearer of this letter to Corinth.[5]
5. Departure from Ephesus, and a ministry at Troas, discontinued when Paul could not find Titus (2 Cor. 2:12-13). Was Paul ill at Troas? (See 2 Cor. 4:17ff.)

2. This unrecorded visit is placed *before* 1 Corinthians by A. Robertson and A. Plummer, *First Epistle of Paul to the Corinthians,* pp. 21-25; and by Henry Alford, *The Greek Testament,* 2:52-54. The visit is placed *after* 1 Corinthians by Merrill Tenney, *New Testament Survey* (Grand Rapids: Eerdmans, 1953), p. 298; and by S. Lewis Johnson, "The First Epistle to the Corinthians," in *The Wycliffe Bible Commentary,* p. 1228. This is one of the unresolved questions.
3. Paul obviously wrote many letters in his lifetime besides those that were "God-breathed" (2 Tim. 3:16).
4. Some view the letter referred to by "I wrote" (1 Cor. 2:4) as being 1 Corinthians, and the sinning brother as the one in 1 Corinthians 5:1-5.
5. Johnson, p. 1228.

6. To Macedonia, for a ministry there (2 Cor. 2:13; Acts 20:1-2).[6] Troubles multiply (2 Cor. 7:5). Titus arrives from Corinth; he shares mixed news:

   (a) of a spiritual awakening in the Corinthian church (2 Cor. 7:6ff.)

   (b) of problems still existing in the church (e.g., 2 Cor. 10:2, 10, 12; 11:4; 12:16, 20-21)

Paul writes 2 Corinthians from Macedonia to prepare the way for his third visit. Titus (with two companions) delivers the epistle to the church (2 Cor. 8:6, 16-24).

7. Paul's final visit to Corinth—three months of ministering (Acts 20:2-3). (See Rom. 16:21-23 for names of Paul's associates at this time.) Paul writes Romans. He escapes a plot against his life (Acts 20:3) and continues on to Jerusalem (Acts 20:3–21:17).

II. THE WRITING OF 2 CORINTHIANS

A. Date

A.D. 56 and 57, depending on how soon after 1 Corinthians (A.D. 55) the letter was written.

B. Place Written

Macedonia (cf. 7:5). One tradition assigns Philippi as the city of origin.

C. Purpose

At least three main purposes can be seen in the epistle:

   (a) to give instruction in doctrine and practical exhortations

   (b) to give further instructions for the offering being gathered for the poor saints in Jerusalem (e.g., 2 Cor. 9:1-5)

   (c) to make an extended defense of Paul's apostleship in view of false accusations by some in the Corinthian church (e.g., 2 Cor. 10:10; 11:13-15; 13:3)

---

6. Paul's *original* plan (cf. 2 Cor. 1:15-16) was to go from Ephesus to Corinth directly by sea, then to Macedonia, then back to Corinth (thus a "second benefit" for the Corinthians, 2 Cor. 1:15), finally on to Jerusalem. His *changed* plan (1 Cor. 16:5-8; Acts 20:3) was to go first to Macedonia, then to Corinth, then to Jerusalem via Macedonia. The reason for delaying his visit to Corinth was to "allow the Corinthians by God's help to remedy the evils, and then to arrive in their midst" (R. C. H. Lenski, *The Interpretation of St. Paul's First and Second Epistles to the Corinthians*, p. 858). One consequence of this change was that the Corinthians charged Paul with not being a man of his word (2 Cor. 1:17).

D. Style and Characteristics

Variety of style is obvious in the epistle. Erasmus describes it this way: "Now he boils up like a limpid spring, suddenly he rolls away with a great noise like a mighty torrent bearing all before it, and then he flows gently along, or expands like a placid lake over all the land."[7] The subject matter usually determines the style. For example, when Paul assumes the role of shepherd of the flock at Corinth, his style is placid and relaxed. When he defends his apostleship, his words rush along like the mighty torrent.

In this "most letter-like of all the letters of Paul,"[8] the apostle is intensely personal, revealing the intimate joys and fears of his tender heart. More is learned about the character and life of an apostle from this epistle than from any other portion of the New Testament.

Contrasts abound in the epistle: glorying and humiliation, life and death, sorrow and consolation, sternness and tenderness. One is aware in reading 2 Corinthians that for Paul the Christian life is all out for Christ or it is not real life at all. The color gray cannot be detected in this book.

E. Unity of the Book

Some modern critics hold that the original 2 Corinthians was not as long as it now stands (e.g., that chaps. 10-13 were not part of the letter).[9] It should be recognized, however, that in no ancient manuscript of this epistle is there "any trace of a division at any point in the letter, or any variation in the arrangement of the material; and in no early Christian writer is there any suggestion that the document is composed of parts of different letters, or that it was not all written at one time to meet one particular situation."[10] In your survey studies of the next lesson you will be observing evidence of a structural unity in the company of diversity of parts.

F. 1 and 2 Corinthians Compared

The following comparisons are suggested by W. Graham Scroggie:[11]

---

7. Quoted by C. F. Kling, *Lange's Commentary on the Holy Scriptures, Corinthians*, p. 5.
8. R. V. G. Tasker, *The Second Epistle of Paul to the Corinthians*, p. 10.
9. For an able defense of the unity of 2 Corinthians, consult Tasker, pp. 23-35.
10. Ibid., pp. 23-24.
11. Adapted from W. Graham Scroggie, *Know Your Bible*, 2:142-43.

11

1 Corinthians	2 Corinthians
objective and practical	subjective and personal
insight into the character of an early church	insight into the character and ministry of Paul
deliberate instruction	impassioned testimony
warns against pagan influences	warns against Judaistic influences

REVIEW QUESTIONS

1. What was the setting of the writing of 1 Corinthians?

What were the main purposes of this first epistle?

2. What was the setting of the writing of 2 Corinthians?

What were its main purposes?

3. One author writes this about 2 Corinthians: "The progress of thought in this epistle is like the movement of a mighty army advancing over rugged terrain still inhabited by pockets of stubborn resistance."[12] What particular subject of the epistle may he have in mind?

12. Wick Broomall, "The Second Epistle to the Corinthians," in *The Wycliffe Bible Commentary*, p. 1261.

Lesson 2
Survey of 2 Corinthians

The skyscraper view of a book of the Bible should always precede the student's ground-level tour. In such a view he is more interested in the *general* layout of the book than in the full details of its individual parts. Large movements, turning points, highlights, and atmosphere are some of the things looked for in survey study. This is the important preliminary work that helps the student become familiar with the book and gives him a feeling of being "at home" when he moves from room to room in the book in the analytical stage.

Approach this eighth book of the New Testament as though you have never seen it before. Keep in mind only the setting of the book, discussed in the previous lesson. For this survey study you might even want to imagine that you are a member of the church at Corinth, reading Paul's letter for the first time. Anything you can do to expose *yourself* to the message of the letter will make spiritual response easier, deeper, and more fruitful.

One of the projects of survey study is to read the entire book in one sitting. Many Bible students shy away from this because they are not accustomed to reading more than a chapter at a time. As one writer says,

> No masterpiece of world-literature has suffered so much by piece-meal reading as the Bible. . . . In Sunday schools it is taught with an equal disregard of book divisions; and even in home study and private reading the same hop-skip-and-jump method is generally followed.[1]

1. C. Alphonso Smith, *What Can Literature Do for Me?* (New York: Doubleday, 1924), pp. 14-15.

13

Even if you do not complete all the exercises of this lesson, be sure to read the thirteen chapters of the epistle in one sitting. You will be glad you did.

I. A FIRST SCANNING

Spend five to ten minutes scanning the entire letter, reading only the first two verses of each paragraph. What does this reveal about the *general* contents of the letter?

_____

Most of the New Testament epistles have the customary opening and closing salutations. Observe the length of these in chapters 1 and 13.

II. A FIRST READING

This is the one-sitting reading that can be completed easily in fifty minutes. Try reading aloud. Don't tarry over any of the details. Read to be impressed. Make mental notes and record some of your impressions.

III. SEGMENT TITLES

Observe on Chart B that 2 Corinthians is divided here into twelve segments (not including the introduction and conclusion). (A segment is a unit of study, usually of a chapter's length. Often it is shorter or longer than a chapter, depending on where the break of the writer's thought appears.) Mark the segment divisions in your Bible. Then read each segment and record a segment title on the chart.[2] (See the two examples.)

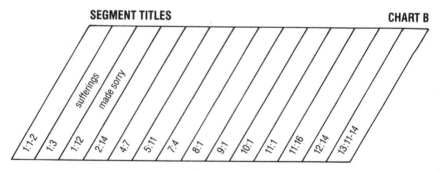

SEGMENT TITLES   CHART B

2. A segment title is a word or phrase taken from the Bible text that is a clue to the main content of the segment. The sum total of titles is *not* intended to be a formal outline of the book.

The locations of divisions not beginning with the first verse of a chapter are based on the following considerations:

1:3-11. This is an opening testimony of Paul. Actually his testimony carries over into the next verses and paragraphs (in fact throughout the epistle), but there appears to be a new beginning at 1:12.

1:12–2:13. Observe the many references to Paul's *coming* to Corinth. This is the main reason for not making a new division at 2:1 but carrying the segment through 2:13.

2:14–4:6. This segment is about Paul's ministry *specifically*, such as preaching (4:5).

4:7–5:10. At 4:7 Paul begins to talk about the "outward man," "earthen vessels," the "body." The subject continues throughout the segment.

5:11–7:3. At 5:11 Paul returns to the subject of ministry, especially the *message* of that ministry ("ministry of reconciliation," 5:18).

7:4-16. Some Bibles make a new paragraph at 7:5 instead of at 7:4.[3] However, in view of the subjects *comfort* and *tribulation* in 7:4, and of the connective "for" in 7:5, it seems better to include 7:4 with the new division.

12:14–13:10. The connecting common phrase is "the third time" (12:14 and 13:1). This is the basis for including 12:14-21 with 13:1-10.

IV. OBSERVATIONS AND OUTLINES

We will use the survey Chart C as the point of reference for the remainder of our studies.[4] Suggestions for study are given below.
1. *Main divisions.* Read chapters 8 and 9 and observe the common subject here. Refer to the survey Chart C and note that this passage is the second of three main divisions in the epistle. Scan chapters 1-7 again, looking for testimonial and doctrinal passages. Then scan chapters 10-13 and observe how frequently Paul defends his apostleship. Read 13:3 for Paul's reasons for devoting four chapters to the subject.

Chart C shows the three main divisions of 2 Corinthians. This much about the structure of the epistle is clear. Beyond this, how-

---

3. Observe, for example, how 7:5 picks up the narrative that had been temporarily suspended at 2:13. It is for this reason that the section 2:14–7:4 is often viewed as a parenthesis in the epistle. More will be said about this later.
4. Advanced students may want to develop their own survey chart in independent study. Help on the survey method of study is given in Irving L. Jensen, *Acts: An Inductive Study* (Chicago: Moody, 1968), pp. 43-54. The analytical chart method is applied throughout the remainder of the book.

ever, it is difficult to find a logical development of the theme of each division that could be represented by any detailed outline.[5] The explanation of this absence of strict logical structure is to be found in the intimate, personal quality of the letter, one that pulsates with emotion. As someone has observed, "Feeling cannot be reduced to system; it vanishes under the dissecting knife."

2. *Kind of content.* Observe the threefold outline: Testimonial and Didactic; Practical; Apologetic.

3. *Paul's ministry.* What are the two main parts of the epistle on this subject?

_____

_____

4. *Tone.* Be alert to change of tone as you move through the epistle.

5. *Biographical setting.* The three main divisions are related to the historical setting. Study the two outlines by T. Zahn that appear at the top of the chart, keeping in mind the setting discussed in the previous lesson. As we have seen, Paul sent this letter to prepare the way for his visit to Corinth, which he wanted to be a success.

6. *Gifts.* The main subject of the central division (chaps. 8-9) is "gifts." Study the outline on the chart. Read the climactic last verse of chapter 9. Observe on the bottom of the chart the epistle's threefold outline on giving and receiving. What is the difference between a gift rejected and a gift received?

_____

_____

Study the outline on "Gifts" developed in chapters 1-7. Observe that while Paul was conscious of trials (e.g., sufferings, sorrow), he never lost sight of gifts from above to help and inspire him in the trial.

7. *Key words and verses.* Note the ones cited on the chart. Read the verses in your Bible. You may want to add to these lists as you move on in your studies.

8. *A title.* The title on the chart reflects the two main subjects of the epistle: *ministry* and *gifts.*

Master the contents of Chart C. Of all the charts in this study manual, you will want to refer most often to this one. Whenever you are analyzing a particular passage, be aware of the context. This is a major contribution of a survey chart.

5. A commendable attempt at outlining is to be found in Alfred Plummer, *Second Epistle of St. Paul to the Corinthians,* pp. 20-21.

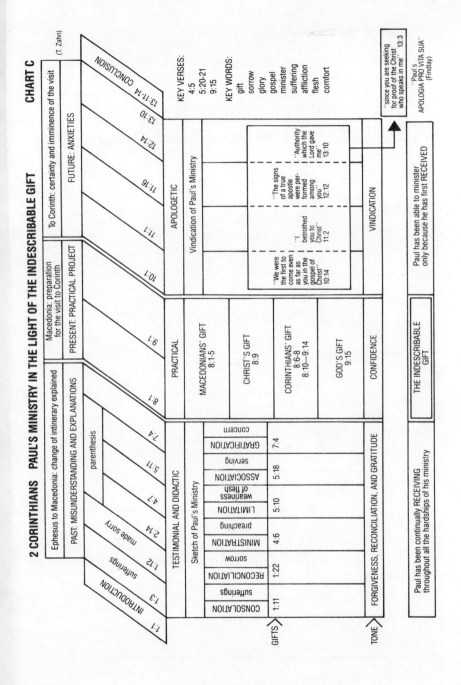

V. IMPORTANT PASSAGES

1. *Important subjects* discussed by Paul in 2 Corinthians include:
   (a) the Old and New covenants contrasted (chap. 3)
   (b) Christ's substitutionary atonement (5:21)
   (c) the gospel of reconciliation (5:18-20)
   (d) separation from worldliness (6:14–7:1)

2. *Key passages* include the following. Read the passages and record the contents:

4:7-12

_____

4:16-18

_____

5:1-10

_____

5:17-21

_____

6:4-10

_____

8:9

_____

9:8

_____

11:23-33

_____

12:1-10

_____

13:14

_____

3. What *autobiographical notes* about Paul do you learn from the following passages?

11:23-27

_____

11:32-33

_____

12:1-4, 7

_____

18

VI. RETROSPECT AND PROSPECT

Do not leave this lesson without thinking back over various verses you have read in your study. Fix in your mind the ones that have stood out for whatever reason. If you are studying in a group, share your impressions with the other members.

Prepare yourself for a closer look at the book as you move into the lessons of *analysis* that follow. Do your studying in utter dependency on the Holy Spirit for illumination to see and understand all that 2 Corinthians has for you.

Lesson 3

2 Corinthians 1:1-11

Comfort in Tribulation

Paul was a giant among men because of his deep gratitude to God and his unselfish consideration of others. Both traits shine forth in the opening eleven verses of 2 Corinthians. The tenderness of the passage is all the more significant when we realize that Paul was writing the letter in trying circumstances. He had just come from what was probably the most excruciating experience of his life (1:8), and he was on his way to a situation in the Corinthian church where opponents were still attacking his apostleship. Keep this in mind as you study the passage.

I. PREPARATION

1. Read the Acts account of some of Paul's trials during his ministry at Ephesus before moving on to Macedonia (Acts 19:9; 19:21–20:1; 20:21; cf. 1 Cor. 15:32). Some expositors think that the "trouble" mentioned in 2 Corinthians 1:8 was one of these trials, through the Corinthian passage describes something more critical than the trials of Acts. Why does God permit unbelievers to attack and oppose Christians to the point of pain? (Cf. Ps. 69; Isa. 43:2; Acts 9:16.)

———————————————————————————

———————————————————————————

2. Read 1 Corinthians 1:1-3 now and refer back to it later when you study the opening salutation of 2 Corinthians 1:1-2.

II. ANALYSIS

Segment to be analyzed: 1:1-11
Paragraph divisions: at verses 1:1, 3, 8 (Mark these in your Bible at the beginning of your study of each lesson.)

A. Salutation: 1:1-2

Break down this concise salutation into two sections of three parts each. Record the phrases below:

The subject	The sender/giver (from)	The object ("unto")
v. 1 This letter, with its greeting (implied)	_____ _____	_____ _____
v.2 _____ and _____	_____ and _____	_____

Make a comparative study of the following words and phrases, looking for any intended shades of meaning:
Office of apostle
"of Jesus Christ":

_____

"by the will of God":

_____

Designations of believers
"brother":

_____

"church of God":

_____

"saints":

_____

(Read 1 Cor. 6:11 to learn who saints are and how they become saints.)
The Godhead
"God":

_____

"our Father":

_____

"the Lord":

_____

"Jesus"(cf. Matt. 1:21):

"Christ" (the word is from *chrio*, "anoint," Luke 4:18):

B. Comfort in Suffering: 1:3-11

Read the two paragraphs (1:3-7; 8-11), underlining key words and phrases in your Bible. Why was the title "Comfort in Suffering" chosen to represent this segment?

Which paragraph is more general, and which is more specific?

Observe the reference to Christ's death in the first paragraph and the reference to His resurrection in the second. Use this observation when you study each paragraph more closely.

1. *Paragraph 1:3-7*
What are the two most repeated words of the paragragh? (Include here *similar* words.)

Study the subject of *suffering* in the paragraph. Observe on Chart C under the segment 1:3-11 the notation of SUFFERINGS. Record what is taught in 1:3-11 about these:
Christ's sufferings

Paul's sufferings

Corinthians' sufferings

How are the three different sufferings related to each other?

Study the subject *comfort* in the paragraph.[1] Record how each of the following is brought into the subject:

1. The words *comfort* and *consolation* translate the same Greek word in these verses.

22

God

_____

Christ

_____

Paul

_____

Corinthians

_____

Note in verse 6 how Paul places affliction and comfort in the same category, as far as a ministry to others is concerned:

"whether we be *afflicted*, it is for your consolation and salvation"

"whether we be *comforted*, it is for your consolation and salvation"

What is Paul trying to get across here?

_____

What does he mean by "salvation"?

_____

_____

2. *Paragraph 1:8-11*

According to these verses, was it physical death that Paul had been delivered from? What is suggested by the statement "we despaired even of life" (1:8)?

_____

What is the dilemma referred to in verse 9?

_____

_____

What is the solution?

_____

_____

Observe the three references to *deliverance* in verse 10. What tenses (past, present, future) are involved?

_____

_____

In verse 11 "gift," which translates the Greek word *charisma*, ap-

23

pears in some versions as "grace."[2] Do you think Paul is referring more to past manifestations of God's grace to him or grace yet to be shown?

III. NOTES

1. *"All the saints which are in all Achaia"* (1:1). Although the primary receivers of Paul's letter were the Corinthians, the letter's audience included believers of other localities in Achaia (Greece). Read Romans 16:1 and Acts 17:34 for references to such places. Do you think Paul ever wrote directly to these groups? If so, why are such letters not part of the New Testament?

2. *"Lord Jesus Christ"* (1:2). Of this designation E. G. Selwyn writes, "The Son is described in three ways: in relationship to us (our *Lord*); in His Person (*Jesus*); and in His divinely-promised and world-wide office (Christ)."[3]

3. *"Father of mercies"* (1:3). *The Wycliffe Bible Commentary* says the word "mercies" is "always in the plural in the N.T. (Rom. 12:1; Phil. 2:1; Col. 3:12; Heb. 10:28)—possibly to express the variegated nature of the virtue."[4]

4. *"Trouble which came to us in Asia"* (1:8). As noted earlier, the trials recorded in Acts 19:21–20:1 do not deem to match the intensity of this "trouble." It could be that Paul had been critically ill. We really do not know what the experience was.

IV. FOR THOUGHT AND DISCUSSION

1. Paul writes, "Sufferings of Christ abound in us" (1:5). What sufferings are meant here? In what sense may they abound in the life of a believer? Should a Christian try to avoid such suffering? Read Hebrews 12:2 in this connection.

2. Observe the two words "sentence" and "trust" in 1:9. Think about various ways these might be compared, in the sense in which Paul uses them in this verse. Why is the life of *trusting* such a glorious one for the Christian?

3. Why is it important that the truths about God's comfort be learned *before* one finds himself in an experience of suffering and affliction? The importance of Bible study is clearly illustrated by this. Read Psalm 119:11 in this connection: "Thy word have I hid

---

2. F. F. Bruce's *Expanded Paraphrase* reads, "Thanks will be given to God by many persons for His grace granted us through the prayer of many."
3. E. G. Selwyn, *The First Epistle of Peter* (New York: Macmillan, 1946), p. 122.
4. Wick Broomall, "The Second Epistle to the Corinthians," p. 1263.

[i.e., treasured up] in my heart, in order that I might not sin against thee." Bible study builds up a treasure or reserve that may be drawn upon for the daily spiritual needs.

4. Make a list of various doctrines and spiritual lessons taught by this passage.

V. FURTHER STUDY

With the help of an exhaustive concordance[5] and a book on word studies,[6] study the words *comfort* and *Christ*. The two vital things to learn about a Bible word are (1) its literal, root meaning; and (2) how the word is used in various passages. Concerning the word *comfort*, study each reference in 2 Corinthians to it and to the other word that translates the same Greek word, *consolation*.

VI. WORDS TO PONDER

I know this: that the more you suffer, the more God will bless you, and help you, and give you His joy (1:7, TLB*).

---

*The Living Bible.

5. Two standard concordances are *Strong's Exhaustive Concordance* and *Young's Analytical Concordance*.

6. An excellent book on New Testament words is W. E. Vine, *An Expository Dictionary of New Testament Words*.

Lesson 4

Maintaining Good Relations with Fellow Christians

Paul knew that if his ministry to the Corinthians was to continue, no opposition could block the way. As of writing this letter, he saw some obstructions ahead. So in his usual frank and kind manner he devotes the second part of his letter (1:12–2:13) to this problem. The title of this lesson is based on Paul's desire to maintain good relations with his brethren at Corinth. He is on his way to visit the Corinthians, and he wants that visit to be a success.

I. PREPARATION FOR ANALYSIS

Review the section of Lesson 1 called The Historical Setting of 2 Corinthians.

1. Some member of the church at Corinth had maliciously heaped some offense upon Paul. It could well be that he was the ringleader of an anti-Paul faction, defying Paul's apostolic authority. This may have taken place during the brief visit that Paul made to Corinth (either before or after writing 1 Corinthians). Relate 2 Corinthians 2:5-1 to this.

2. Paul wrote at least two noncanonical letters to the Corinthians before writing 2 Corinthians. One of these is referred to in 2 Corinthians 2:3-4, 9.

3. Paul's trip to Macedonia *before* making a planned visit to Corinth was the outcome of a change of plans. Some Corinthians felt slighted by this. Relate 2 Corinthians 1:15-17 to this change of plan.

4. Titus was probably one of the bearers of 1 Corinthians to the church at Corinth, and he may have been the bearer of the "painful" letter written soon thereafter. Paul anxiously awaited Titus's return from Corinth so that he could learn how his letters were received. Relate 2 Corinthians 2:12-13.

II. ANALYSIS

Segment to be analyzed: 1:12–2:13
Paragraph divisions: at verses 1:12, 15, 23; 2:5, 12

A. General Analysis

There are many important spiritual lessons in this passage, taken from real-life situations in the experiences of Paul and the Corinthians. In your analysis of the text recognize the background and setting reviewed above, and the spiritual lessons will stand out all the more.

Chart D is a work sheet for the five paragraphs of 1:12–2:13. After you have read the segment once, observe the following on the chart:

1. The title represents Paul's main purpose in writing this segment. Compare the *Today's English Version* reading of 1:12*b* with that of the King James.

2. Read each paragraph again, observing how each is represented in the following outline:
The Relationship Described
Clarification of a Misunderstanding
An Appeal
An Explanation

3. Complete the outline of *Traits of Paul*. (Examples are given.)

4. Use the blank spaces on the work sheet to record various observations and outlines as you proceed with your more detailed analysis.

B. Paragraph Analysis

1. *Paragraph 1:12-14*: The Relationship Described.
Read this paragraph in various modern versions. You will notice different readings for these King James renderings. (See chart on next page.)
Keep in mind these different renderings as you analyze the paragraph. What do verses 12 and 14 teach about Paul's relationship to the Corinthians *in the past*?

What is the reference to *present* in verse 13?

27

King James	Modern Versions (some examples)
"rejoicing" (1:12, 14)	"boasting"
"simplicity" (1:12)	"holiness"[1]
"conversation" (1:12)	"behavior"
"acknowledge" (1:13-14)	"understand," "accept"
"to the end" (1:13)	"fully"

What is the reference to *future* in verses 13 and 14?

What is so healthy about the testimony of a good conscience (1:12)?

How would you contrast these two kinds of behavior (1:12):
    (a) with fleshly wisdom
    (b) by the grace of God
    To help you identify what Paul is referring to by "day of the Lord Jesus" (1:14), read 1 Corinthians 1:8; 5:5; Philippians 1:6, 10; 1 Thessalonians 5:2; 2 Thessalonians 2:2.
2. *Paragraph 1:15-22:* Stability of the Changed Plan.
Study the parts of this paragraph in this order:
(a) *The original plan* (1:15-16). What was this plan according to these verses?

Read the word "before" (v. 15) as "first" (Berkeley).
(b) *The changed plan* (Read 1:23 for a reference to this). What was the change?

(c) *The resultant question* (1:17). Paul's rhetorical questions reveal the accusation that his opponents were making against him. What was that?

For the sake of clarity, read "yea, yea, and nay, nay" as "yea, when I really mean no."[2]

---

1. This rendering is based on a different manuscript reading than the one translated "simplicity."
2. See *The Living Bible.*

PAUL MAINTAINING GOOD RELATIONS WITH THE CORINTHIANS 1:12—2:13

"our lives in this world, and especially our relations with you'" (1:12b, TEV)

THE RELATIONSHIP DESCRIBED	CLARIFICATION OF A MISUNDERSTANDING		AN APPEAL	AN EXPLANATION
	PROPOSED VISIT TO CORINTH			TRAITS OF PAUL
	stability of the changed plan	reason for the changed plan		
1:12	1:15	1:23	2:5	2:12	2:13
SIMPLICITY AND GODLY SINCERITY	STABILITY AND CONSISTENCY			

29

(d) *Paul's reply* (1:18). Paul takes his stand on what appears to be an oath. (Cf. 1:23). What is he really saying?

_____

_____

(e) *No vacillating in the Godhead* (1:19-22). This is the solid doctrinal part of the paragraph. What does Paul write about the following:
(1) the Son of God (v. 19):

_____

(2) the promises of God (v. 20):

_____

(3) the works of God (vv. 21-22):

_____

How does Paul relate himself to this bedrock foundation?

_____

How does he thereby relate his changed plan to it?

_____

3. *Paragraph 1:23–2:4*: Reason for the Changed Plan.
According to 7:12, what was Paul's letter (referred to in this paragraph) about? Why was it written?

_____

Why did Paul delay his visit to Corinth?

_____

_____

How would a delay help to make his visit a joyous one?

_____

_____

Compare these phrases: (a) "not ... dominion over your faith" and (b) "but ... helpers of your joy" (1:24).
   Which of the following two modern paraphrases do you think is closer to what Paul means in verse 24:
   (a) "For though I am not responsible for your faith—your standing in God is your own affair—yet I can add to your happiness" (Phillips).
   (b) "Although I can't do much to help your faith, for it is strong already, I want to be able to do something about your joy ..."(TLB).

In this paragraph Paul is demonstrating his love and concern for the Corinthians. Keep this in mind as you move to the next paragraph, where Paul appeals to the Corinthians to show love to a sinner in their midst.

4. *Paragraph 2:5-11*: An Appeal.

The letter referred to in the previous paragraph was in part written about the offender of this paragraph. Paul has some important things to say here about how a Christian group should deal with an offense committed by one of its members. What is the tone of Paul's appeal?

_____

This reading of 2:5-7a will clarify some hazy phrases of the King James: "If someone has caused grief, he has not simply grieved me but, to some extent at least—not to exaggerate—all of you. For such a one this censure by the majority suffices; so, instead of further rebuke, you should forgive. . . ."[3]

Whatever was the sin of the offender, it affected Paul especially and also the whole congregation at Corinth. Study this paragraph for the important truths that it teaches concerning the following:

(a) what sin inflicts upon others (v. 5):

_____

(b) who may be affected by another's sin (v. 5):

_____

(c) what the offender reaps (vv. 6-7):

_____

(d) what the offended or es owe the offender (vv. 7-10):

_____

(e) individual and corporate forgiveness (v. 10):

_____

(f) basis of forgiveness (v. 10):

_____

(g) the tragic consequences of a nonforgiving spirit (v. 11):

_____

5. *Paragraph 2:12-13*: An Explanation.

Note the two geographical names. One writer remarks, "The whole epistle is an itinerary. The very stages of his journey are impressed upon it: the troubles at Ephesus, the repose at Troas, the

3. Berkeley Version.

anxiety and consolation of Macedonia, the prospect of moving to Corinth."[4] The touchy word of this short paragraph is "Macedonia." It was Paul's going to Macedonia first, rather than to Corinth first, that offended the Corinthians. Paul wrote these lines to explain what it was that gave him assurances as to where he should be at any given moment. Observe how his experiences illustrate these principles:

(a) The need of a city to hear the gospel is not of itself the determinant of place of ministry, or Paul would have remained at Troas (v. 12*a*).

(b) An open door of witnessing is not of itself this determinant (v. 12*b*).[5]

(c) Constant rest in one's spirit is the still, small voice of this assurance of being in the Lord's place (v. 13). Obviously such peace of mind comes only to one who is in close fellowship with God. Read again 1:21-22 and you will understand more clearly why in the context of those verses Paul identified his life and calling with God.

The next reference to Macedonia in this epistle is at 7:5. Read this verse and the ones that follow, and you will see the sequel to this "rest of spirit" experience of Paul. (As indicated in the survey Lesson 2, 2:14–7:4 may be viewed as a parenthesis in the ongoing theme of the epistle.)

III. NOTES

1. *"Sincerity"* (1:12). The word has either of these connotations: (a) that which is tested by sunlight and found to be unstained; (b) one pure substance, unadulterated, unalloyed.

2. *"Amen"* (1:20). An "Amen" spoken by God means "Thus it shall be." An "Amen" spoken by man means "So let it be." Read Revelation 22:20. Truth and trustworthiness are inherent in the word.

3. *"Earnest"* (1:22). The word means "guarantee." In New Testament times it was used of the down payment made for a purchase, guaranteeing that the balance would be forthcoming. A correct translation of "the earnest of the Spirit" is "the guarantee which is the Spirit." Read the other two places in the New Testament where the word appears: 2 Corinthians 5:5; Ephesians 1:14.

4. A. Bengel, quoted in Marvin R. Vincent, *Word Studies in the New Testament*, 3:297.
5. G. Campbell Morgan identifies the open door not with a ministry in Troas but with an opportunity to go to Corinth: "He came to Troas, saw the open door to Corinth, but did not enter it" (*The Corinthian Letters of Paul*, p. 153).

4. *"Also did I write"* (2:9). This is the same letter referred to in 2:3-4.

IV. FOR THOUGHT AND DISCUSSION

1. How do these qualities manifest themselves in everyday Christian living: simplicity, godly sincerity, grace of God?

2. Is it right for a Christian to be motivated in his conduct by the assurance of a coming day of the Lord when, among other things, there will be rewards and judgment?

3. How can a Christian know he is in the will of God when a change of plans is involved?

4. What are some genuine evidences of concern and passion for others in their needs?

5. What is genuine forgiveness? Is it possible to fulfill the spirit of the slogan "Forgive and forget"?

6. From your knowledge of Scripture (and from your own experiences) what are some of the ways and methods of Satan used against Christians?

7. Read Acts 20:6 concerning Paul's later ministry at Troas. Do you think God gave this opportunity of service to Paul to make up for the earlier cancellation (2 Cor. 2:12-13)?

V. FURTHER STUDY

1. The name of Titus does not appear in the book of Acts, and yet he was a close associate of Paul. Consult a Bible dictionary for a biographical sketch of the young man.[6]

2. Three recommended word studies are on the words "forgive," "amen," and "Satan."

VI. WORDS TO PONDER

We don't want Satan to win any victory here, and well we know his methods! (2:11, Phillips).

---

6. An excellent article on Titus may be found in Merrill F. Unger, *Unger's Bible Dictionary.*

The Ministry of Proclaiming Christ

Paul's first love was to preach the gospel of his Lord and Saviour, Jesus Christ. God gave him this passion when he was first saved. Preaching was not *his* choice, but *God's*. Acts 9:15 reports the clear statement of this divine call: "He is a chosen vessel unto me, to bear my name before the Gentiles, and kings, and the children of Israel." In the passage of this lesson we will be reading some of Paul's reflections about this ministry of proclaiming Christ. If he loved *to preach*, he was no less enthusiastic in talking *about preaching*. Among his reasons for sharing these things with the Corinthians at this time are:

1. Their first contact with him was through his preaching.

2. His apostleship (and therefore his apostolic preaching) was being challenged by some of them.

3. He wanted to magnify the Person of his preaching and clarify the methods of his preaching.

4. He wanted the Corinthians to learn important spiritual lessons applicable to laymen as well as to preachers, since both are witnesses of the gospel.

I. PREPARATION FOR ANALYSIS

1. Refer to the survey Chart C again and review the context of 2:14–4:6. As was noted earlier, the section 2:14–7:3 could be viewed as a parenthesis in the sense that its content is mainly topical, not biographical like its surrounding sections. This is shown of Chart E. (Read the verses in your Bible.)

The common subject of 2:14–7:3 is the *ministry* of Paul. Tenney breaks down this section into the outline on the following page:[1]

---

1. Merrill Tenney, *New Testament Survey*, p. 300.

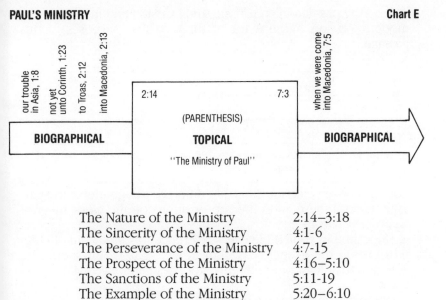

The Nature of the Ministry	2:14–3:18
The Sincerity of the Ministry	4:1-6
The Perseverance of the Ministry	4:7-15
The Prospect of the Ministry	4:16–5:10
The Sanctions of the Ministry	5:11-19
The Example of the Ministry	5:20–6:10
The Appeal of the Ministry	6:11–7:4

2. Read Exodus 34:20-35 for the interesting story of Moses and the veil. Paul uses this narrative to illustrate some important truths about communication of the gospel.

II. ANALYSIS

Segment to be analyzed: 2:14–4:6. (This may be broken down into two smaller units for study: 2:14–3:11 and 3:12–4:6.)
Paragraph divisions: at verses 2:14, 16*b*; 3:7, 12; 4:1

A. General Analysis

1. First mark the paragraph divisions in your Bible. Bible versions differ in the first half of the segment as to where new paragraphs should begin. This is because clear changes of subject (which are the reasons for new paragraphs) are not always evident here. The important thing for your individual study is to work with just *one* set of paragraph divisions, wherever the divisions are made. Reasons for the divisions given above will become apparent in the course of your analysis.

2. Read the passage in your basic study version and in at least one modern version. Write a list of three to five purposes of this passage.

---

3. What is Paul's overall mood as he writes here?

You may observe various tones in different paragraphs of the passage. Record these and other observations on the work sheet of analytical Chart F.
4. Underline in your Bible every reference to some form of *communicating* the gospel (e.g., "speak we," 2:17). You should be able to find at least one reference per paragraph. Record these on Chart F.
5. Compare the beginning and ending of the segment.

---

6. Note the main topical study shown on Chart F with the master title, "Preachers of the Gospel." What phrase in the Bible text of each paragraph is the basis for each of the five paragraph points? Record each phrase at the end of each arrow on the chart. Try making your own topical study, similar to this. Various studies of this kind are usually obtainable in any one passage of Scripture. How can such outlines be used in preaching and teaching ministries?

B. Paragraph Analysis

1. *Paragraph 2:14-16*a: Sweet Savor unto God.
What is the key repeated word of the paragraph?

What does the word mean?

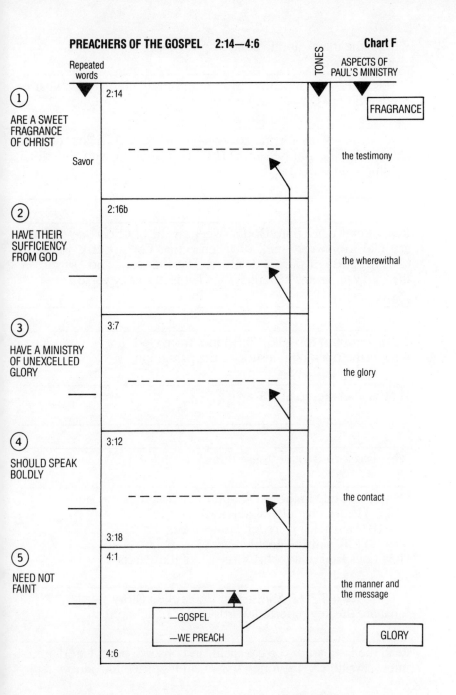

PREACHERS OF THE GOSPEL   2:14—4:6

Repeated words

TONES

Chart F

ASPECTS OF PAUL'S MINISTRY

FRAGRANCE

① ARE A SWEET FRAGRANCE OF CHRIST

Savor

2:14

the testimony

② HAVE THEIR SUFFICIENCY FROM GOD

2:16b

the wherewithal

③ HAVE A MINISTRY OF UNEXCELLED GLORY

3:7

the glory

④ SHOULD SPEAK BOLDLY

3:12

3:18

the contact

⑤ NEED NOT FAINT

4:1

the manner and the message

—GOSPEL

—WE PREACH

4:6

GLORY

37

What is the translation in a modern version?

_____

Observe the two appearances of the phrase "unto God." What is rendered unto God in each case?

_____

Refer to the *Notes* for the background to verse 14. What do you learn from the phrase "in Christ" as it appears with the word "triumph" in verse 14?

_____

Read "For we are unto God a sweet savour of Christ" as "For we are like the sweet smell of incense that Christ burns to God" (TEV*). Read "savour of death" as "fatal aroma," and "savour of life" as "vital aroma" (Berkeley). What is meant by verse 16?

_____

2. *Paragraph 2:16b–3:6*: Sufficiency from God.
What is the opening question of the paragraph?

_____

How is it answered in 3:5-6?

_____

What is referred to by "these things" (v. 16*b*)?

_____

Observe a unity in the paragraph as indicated by this outline:
    (a) Paul's unadulterated preaching (2:17)
    (b) Paul's living credentials (3:1-3)
    (c) Paul's divine enablement (3:4-6)
How does Paul relate Christ to each of these facts?

_____

3. *Paragraph 3:7-11*: Ministry of Unexcelled Glory.
What are the key repeated words of this paragraph?

_____

Read the last part of verse 6 again, and observe how "letter" introduces "written . . . in stones" (v. 7), and "spirit"[2] introduces "spir-

Today's English Version.
2. Most modern translations show the word in these verses as Spirit, not spirit.

it" (v. 8). (Cf. also v. 3b.) What is Paul comparing throughout the paragraph? Record the various comparisons made (example given).

Verse	OLD COVENANT Former Ministry of Glory	NEW COVENANT Present Ministry of Glory	Comparison Made
7-8	—death —written in stones —glory faded away	—Spirit	—more glorious
9-10			
11			

By making these comparisons is Paul implying that the law was of no value?

_____

What was the purpose of the law? (Cf. Rom. 7:7ff.; Gal. 3:19-22.)

_____

_____

4. *Paragraph 3:12-18*: Ministry of Unveiled Glory.
What is the key repeated word of the paragraph?

_____

Why had Moses put a veil on his face?

_____

(Note this reading of 3:13: "He put a veil on his face, to prevent the Israelites from gazing until they saw the end of a glory which was to vanish away."[3] Cf. the glory "done away" in 3:7; also cf. Ex. 34:30.) Paul emphasizes in this paragraph that such a veil is "done away in Christ" (3:14). What does this mean for the Christian? Look at verses 17 and 18 for answers to this. Reading a paraphrased New Testament will also help.

_____

_____

3. Bruce's *Expanded Paraphrase.*

39

How does Paul apply this truth of unveiled glory to his preaching ministry? (See v. 12, where the phrase "plainness of speech" means "boldness.")

5. *Paragraph 4:1-6*: A Persevering Ministry.
Throughout the segment of 2:14–4:6, Paul is conscious of *what he has* from God. In the first paragraph (2:14-16*a*) it is *triumph*. In the second (2:16*b*–3:6), it is *sufficiency*. The opening phrase of 3:12, which refers back to paragraph 3:7-11, says "we have *such hope*." The opening phrase of 4:1, which refers to the preceding verses, says "we have *this ministry*." refer to the text of 3:12 and 4:1, and complete the statement by including the "therefore":
3:12—We have *such hope*; therefore

4:1—We have *such a ministry*; therefore

What truths can you find in this paragraph that are causes for persevering in the ministry of proclaiming Christ?

Various doctrines are taught in this paragraph. It is difficult to identify any one doctrine as the prominent one. Analyze the paragraph carefully and try to arrive at some outline. Here is an example of an outline centered on the subject of the gospel:
Witness of the Gospel
Intended Hearers of the Gospel
Person of the Gospel.
What phrases in the paragraph stand out as key ones?

Relate Paul's testimony "God . . . hath shined in our hearts" (v. 6) to his initial experience of conversion (Acts 26:13-18).

What does this last phrase say to you: "the glory of God in the face of Jesus Christ"?

_____

_____

III. NOTES

1. *"Causeth us to triumph"* (2:14). Most versions read this as "leads us in triumph." Many expositors see this as a reference to a military general leading a train of captives into a city.[4] However, Paul does not seem to be bringing in the idea of captivity here, even though it is true that Christians are bondslaves of Christ. Bruce's excellent translation of this verse is, "Now thanks be to God, who always gives us a place of honour in Christ's triumphal procession!" *(Expanded Paraphrase).*

2. *"In Christ"* (2:14). This phrase (and similar ones) occurs over fifty times in the New Testament, nearly every time in Paul's writings. Union with Christ underlies all the other doctrines expounded by the apostle.

3. *"Sufficient"* (2:16). The word is variously translated as "capable," "qualified," "equal to the responsibility." It is derived from a Greek root meaning "to arrive."

4. *"Corrupt the word of God"* (2:17). This is the only New Testament verse where this word translated "corrupt" appears. The Greek word is derived from *kapēlos* ("huckster", "peddler"), a term that "especially applied to retailers of wine, with whom adulteration and short measure were matters of course."[5] See Isaiah 1:22 for a reference to this kind of adulteration.

5. *"Epistle of Christ ministered by us, written . . . with the Spirit"* (3:3). The Corinthian Christians were the "epistle"; the "author" of the epistle was Christ; the "pen" was Paul; and the "ink" was the Holy Spirit.

6. *"Ministration of condemnation"* (3:9). Morgan compares the Old and New covenants thus: "The letter [law] reveals, and so condemns. The Spirit realizes, that is, communicates life."[6] As to the exposing ministry of the law, read Romans 5:20; 7:7-13.

7. *"Ministration of righteousness"* (3:9). The *Expanded Paraphrase* translates this as "ministry of justification."[7] The Greek words for "righteousness" and "justification" have the same root meaning.

4. Marvin R. Vincent, *Word Studies in the New Testament*, 3:298.
5. Ibid., p. 300.
6. G. Campbell Morgan, *The Corinthian Letters of Paul*, p. 154.
7. Another modern translation reads "service by which we are declared innocent" (TEV). This is a definition of justification.

8. *"Even unto this day, when Moses is read, the veil is upon their [the Jews'] heart"* (3:15). Tasker observes that "few passages in the New Testament emphasize more strongly than this that the Old Testament Scriptures are only fully intelligible when Christ is seen to be their fulfilment."[8]

9. *"There is liberty"* (3:17). Paul concludes the sentence with this word "liberty" without dwelling on its application. *The Living Bible* suggests an application, in view of the preceding context, by adding: "There is freedom [from trying to be saved by keeping the laws of God]." Read the following verses to see various kinds of bondage from which the believer is set free: Galatians 5:18; Romans 7:6; 8:15, 21, 23.

10. *"Beholding as in a glass"* (3:18). The word "glass" is best rendered "mirror." Expositors and translators are divided as to whether the translation should be "beholding" or "reflecting." Tasker rightly comments, "Whatever may be the exact significance of this difficult word, the main emphasis in the verse is upon the transformation in the Christian as he contemplates the glory of God on the face of Jesus Christ."[9]

IV. FOR THOUGHT AND DISCUSSION

1. In what ways can a Christian's life be like sweet, fragrant incense rising to God?

2. "To those who are not being saved, we [Christians] seem a fearful smell of death and doom" (2:16*a*, TLB). What did Paul mean by this? Have you ever had the experience of having unbelievers look upon you in this way?

3. How is the message of the Bible being diluted, corrupted (2:17), and handled deceitfully (4:2) by individuals and groups today?

4. What important lessons have you learned from this passage about *the Christian life as a good witness of Jesus Christ?*

V. FURTHER STUDY

1. Make a comparative study of law and Spirit as taught in Romans 7 and Galatians 3.

2. Study what the Bible teaches about God's glory and the believer's relationship to that glory. (A quick glance at a concordance will reveal that this important word appears in most of the books of the Bible.)

8. R. V. G. Tasker, *The Second Epistle of Paul to the Corinthians*, p. 66.
9. Ibid., p. 68.

VI. WORDS TO PONDER

We do not advertise ourselves, but we proclaim Christ Jesus as Lord; as for us, we present ourselves to you as your servants for Jesus' sake (4:5, *Expanded Paraphrase*).

Lesson 6

God's Treasure in Common Clay Vessels

In our last lesson we learned how thrilled Paul was to be a witness for Jesus Christ. That was Paul the Christian enthusiast. In this lesson we meet Paul the Christian realist, as he reflects honestly on the constant mundane pressures and restrictions of performing the glorious *divine calling* in a frail *human body*.

The bright aspect of this passage is not only Paul's honesty but his triumphant spirit. Paul was not a pessimist or a fatalist. He faced problems and circumstances squarely and did not flinch, because his eyes were on Jesus, Master and Conqueror of all. If God chose to deposit His treasures in common, clay vessels, Paul was perfectly satisfied to leave the outcome with Him. Your study of this passage of 2 Corinthians could be the most fruitful one for you personally as you learn Paul's "secret" of such a victorious spirit.

I. PREPARATION FOR ANALYSIS

1. Bear in mind the subject of Lesson 5, where Paul's preaching ministry was described. Recall the bright words penned by the apostle, such as triumph, savor, life, sufficiency, glory. Consider again how the passage of the last lesson ended—on the effulgent splendor of "the glory of God in the face of Jesus Christ" (4:6). Now read the first part of verse 7. What does the first word suggest?

The phrase "this treasure" refers to what Paul has been talking about in the preceding passage. What is that?

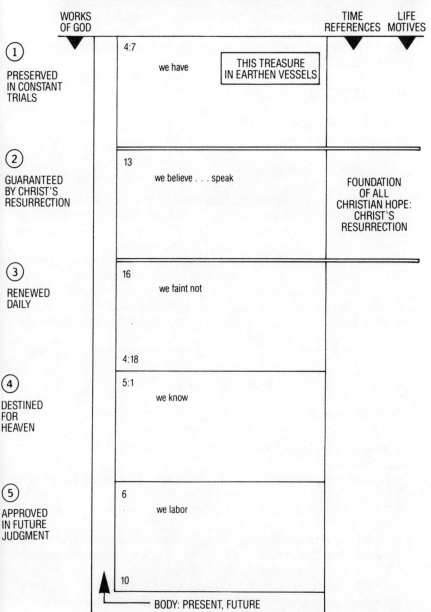

EARTHEN VESSELS BEARING GOD'S TREASURE   4:7—5:10   **Chart G**

WORKS OF GOD   TIME REFERENCES   LIFE MOTIVES

①
PRESERVED
IN CONSTANT
TRIALS

4:7   we have   THIS TREASURE IN EARTHEN VESSELS

②
GUARANTEED
BY CHRIST'S
RESURRECTION

13   we believe . . . speak

FOUNDATION
OF ALL
CHRISTIAN HOPE:
CHRIST'S
RESURRECTION

③
RENEWED
DAILY

16   we faint not

4:18

④
DESTINED
FOR
HEAVEN

5:1   we know

⑤
APPROVED
IN FUTURE
JUDGMENT

6   we labor

10

BODY: PRESENT, FUTURE

45

In what sense is it a *treasure?*

2. In anticipation of Paul's Old Testament quotation in 4:13, read Psalm 116. The verse quoted is verse 10. Study the whole psalm as the surrounding context of verse 10. Note references to death, such as verse 15.

II. ANALYSIS

Segment to be analyzed: 4:7–5:10
Paragraph divisions: at verses 4:7, 13, 16; 5:1, 6

A. General Analysis

1. After you have marked the paragraph divisions in your Bible, read the segment once or twice. Underline every reference to the human body, such as synonyms (e.g., "tabernacle"), descriptions ("persecuted"), destiny ("death"), and similar aspects. Record these in the paragraph boxes of Chart G. It will become obvious from this exercise what the segment's main subject is.
2. For each paragraph, record in the narrow vertical column whether the emphasis is on the present body or the future body.
3. What basic Christian doctrine is stated in the second paragraph?

_____

Why is this doctrine basic?

_____

4. Scan the segment for every reference to *time.* Record these on the chart.
5. Note every reference to God, Christ, the Holy Spirit. Record the *Works of God.*
6. Life motives appear throughout the segment. Locate each reference.
7. Read the outline shown on the chart, under the master title *Earthen Vessels Bearing God's Treasure.* Check each paragraph to see how each paragraph point (shown in the left-hand margin) was derived. Try making your own topical study for this segment.
8. By now you have become well acquainted with the segment as a whole. With that hold on the passage, move now to the more detailed analysis of each paragraph. Keep your eyes continually trained to look for new things.

46

B. Paragraph Analysis

1. *Paragraph 4:7-12*: Preserved in Constant Trials.
Because the entire segment is a study of contrasts and comparisons, the word "but" appears frequently.[1] Observe in this paragraph the occurrences of the words "but" and "yet." Record the sets of contrasts in verses 8 and 9:

WE ARE	WE ARE NOT

How can a Christian be troubled on every side and yet not be distressed?

_____

What is Paul's answer to this in verse 10 and 11?

_____

What is the repeated statement at the end of each of these verses?

_____

Analyze verse 7 carefully. What is the contrast in the phrase "treasure in earthen vessels"?

_____

_____

Why did God choose to let the proclamation of the gospel be accomplished in weak, breakable, common vessels (v. 7*b*)? Read 1 Corinthians 1:26-29.

_____

_____

---

1. *The Wycliffe Bible Commentary* (pp. 1269-70) lists these pairs in the first part of this passage (4:7-18): frail and mighty (4:7); trials and triumphs (4:8-10); death and life (4:11-12); the written and the spoken (4:13); the past and the future (4:14); grace and thanksgiving (4:15); outer and inner man (4:16); affliction and glory (4:17); seen and unseen (4:18*a*); temporal and eternal (4:18*b*).

What do you think Paul means by verse 12? (See *Notes.*)

_____

_____

2. *Paragraph 4:13-15:* Guaranteed by Christ's resurrection.
What grand miracle is stated as a fact in verse 14?

_____

What miracle in the experience of believers is guaranteed by this?

_____

What is the key repeated word of verse 13?

_____

Can the *fact* of Christ's resurrection be personally appropriated if
there is no *faith?*

_____

_____

Also, can there be an Easter *faith* without the Easter *fact?*

_____

Note how the last phrase of verse 13 extends the thought to a third
point:

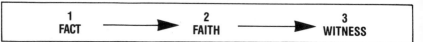

Review your study of Psalm 116 at this point. Morgan's counsel to
prospective ministers was, "If you do not believe, do not talk."
   The reading of verse 15 in the King James is heavy and not
entirely clear. Most modern versions read something like the
paraphrase of *The Living Bible.* "These sufferings of ours are for
your benefit. And the more of you who are won to Christ, the
more there are to thank Him for His great kindness, and the more
the Lord is glorified."
3. *Paragraph 4:16-18:* Renewed Daily.
Study the contrasts made in the paragraphs after you have recorded them on the chart on the following page.
What does this testimony reveal about Paul?

_____

_____

outward man	
perish	
light	
affliction	
for a moment	
seen	
temporal	
	"That is why we never give up" (4:16a, Living Bible.)

4. *Paragraph 5:1-5*: Destined for Heaven.
Read the paragraph. Then determine the intended reference of each of these metaphors:
(a) earthly house of this tabernacle (tent) (5:1):

_____

(b) house from heaven (5:2):

_____

(c) dissolved (5:1):

_____

(d) groan (5:2, 4):

_____

(e) clothed upon (5:2-3):

_____

Paul is comparing two bodies. What bodies are these?

_____

Does Paul write here about the intermediate state (between death and the rapture) of a deceased believer?

_____

Is there any specific reference to the Lord's return?

_____

What is Paul's main point in this paragraph?

_____

On the meaning of verse 3, see *Notes*. Relate the first three words of the paragraph ("For we know") to the concluding phrase ("earnest of the Spirit)." How is the Holy Spirit a pledge of things to come?

_____

_____

5. *Paragraph 5:6-10*: Approved in Future Judgment.
Paul's desire is not only to go to heaven but to be approved of God when he reaches heaven. How are these two thoughts expressed in the paragraph?

_____

Observe every verb in the paragraph whose subject is "we." Make a study of these.
The judgment seat (Greek, *bema*, "platform") of Christ is for what purpose?

_____

Compare 1 Corinthians 3:10-15, which clearly teaches exact retribution for Christians. In what sense would it be true to say that a Christian is determining, at least in part, what his life in heaven will be by how he lives on earth?

_____

Who are the "we . . . all," in view of the context of the paragraph?

_____

How does this future judgment motivate Paul (v. 9)?

_____

III. NOTES

1. *"Earthen vessels"* (4:7). Such vessels were made of burnt clay, "cheap, utterly common, the least valued, used with small care, bound to break sooner or later."[2] Lenski comments on the treasure so deposited: "The astonishing thing is that such a divine treasure, God's own presence of grace, the ultimate of what is heavenly, absolutely priceless, beyond the value of all rubies and

_____

2. R. C. H. Lenski, *The Interpretation of St. Paul's First and Second Epistle to the Corinthians*, p. 974.

50

diamonds of earth, should be placed into such wretched vessels and be kept in them so long."[3]

2. *"Death worketh in us, but life in you"* (4:12). Tasker interprets Paul as meaning that "because his sufferings afford evidence of the risen power of Jesus, they are a source of life, to those to whom he ministers, the life that can be found in Jesus alone."[4]

3. *"If so be that being clothed we shall not be found naked"* (5:3). Much space is devoted in commentaries to this difficult verse. Lenski translates the verse thus: "Since also, after having put it on, we shall be found not naked." (TEV has the same sense.) Paul was assured that the unclothing process of death would not leave him "naked," for he had a sure hope of everlasting habitation.

4. *"Accepted of him"* (5:9). Read the following verses where the Greek word for "accepted" appears: Romans 12:1-2; 14:18; Ephesians 5:10; Philippians 4:18; Colossians 3:20; Titus 2:9; Hebrews 13:21.

5. *"Judgment seat of Christ"* (5:10). This judgment is not to be confused with the great white throne judgment at the end of time (Rev. 20:11-15), before which only unbelievers shall appear. The "bema" judgment of Christ (2 Cor. 5:10) is a judgment of believers' works, which will take place in heaven after the saints have been raptured.

IV. FOR THOUGHT AND DISCUSSION

1. What does it mean for a Christian to bear about in his body the dying of Jesus (4:10)? Compare Romans 8:36; 1 Corinthians 15:31; Galatians 6:17; Colossians 1:24. How is Christ's life manifested in a Christian when His dying is borne? (Cf. Gal. 2:20; Phil. 1:20.)

2. How can suffering, including physical suffering, make a Christian's testimony more vibrant? Refer to Lesson 3 and recall what you learned there about a Christian's experiences in suffering.

3. One of the earlier exercises of this lesson was to look in the passage for motives for Christian living. Think more about this and about how your own life is geared to these.

V. FURTHER STUDY

Make a topical study of judgment for Christians, as taught in the

3. Ibid.
4. R. V. G. Tasker, *The Second Epistle of Paul to the Corinthians*, p. 74.

New Testament. Various outside helps will direct you to the passages involved.[5]

VI. WORDS TO PONDER

That is why we never give up. It is hard on our health, but good for our souls. Down inside we grow stronger in the Lord every day (4:16, TLB).

---

5. For example, *Nave's Topical Bible.*

Lesson 7

2 Corinthians 5:11–7:3

An Ambassador for Christ

This lesson covers the third and last part of the parenthesis 2:14–7:3 on the gospel's ministry. In the first segment (2:14–4:6) the emphasis was on the *speaking* aspect of the ministry. In 4:7–5:10 the subject was the *broadcasting channel* of the ministry—the astounding fact that God has committed the proclamation of the gospel to frail humans—"treasure in earthen vessels." In the passage of this lesson Paul relates his ministry to the Corinthians more intimately and personally. He is Christ's *ambassador to them*, God speaking to them through him (5:20). It is in this passage (the only occurrence in the Corinthian letters[1]) that the phrase appears "O ye Corinthians" (6:11). The atmosphere of the entire segment is well captured by this paraphrase of 6:11: "Oh, my dear Corinthian friends! I have told you all my feelings; I love you with all my heart."[2]

I. PREPARATION FOR ANALYSIS

1. Review your studies of the last two lessons, recalling what Paul has written since 2:14 on the subject of the ministry of the gospel.

2. Read Isaiah 49:8 in its context, in anticipation of its quote in 2 Corinthians 6:2. Also read Exodus 25:8; 29:45; Leviticus 26:11ff.; Jeremiah 31:1; Ezekiel 36:27; and Isaiah 52:11 for background to the quotes of 6:16 and 6:17.

3. A comparison of the three segments of the parenthesis 2:14–7:3 is shown on Chart H. Fix this in your mind now as you prepare to analyze the third segment.

---

1. Compare similar readings in Galatians 3:1 and Philippians 4:15.
2. *The Living Bible.*

53

THE MINISTRY OF THE GOSPEL			
2:14	4:7	5:11	7:3
GLORIOUS NATURE of the Gospel	FRAIL BEARERS of the Gospel	BELOVED HEARERS of the Gospel	

II. ANALYSIS

Segment to be analyzed: 5:11–7:3
Paragraph divisions: at verses 5:11, 16; 6:1, 11, 14; 7:2

A. General Analysis

1. After you have marked the paragraph divisions in your Bible, read the segment a few times, looking for the following. (Mark observations in your Bible whenever possible.)
    (a) things that especially stand out, for whatever reason
    (b) every reference to the ministry of the gospel (e.g., "we persuade men," 5:11)
    (c) every reference to Paul's *personal* ministry and relationship to the Corinthians
    (d) the main point of each paragraph
    (e) which paragraphs contain mainly testimony and doctrine
    (f) which paragraphs contain mainly command and exhortation
2. Compare paragraphs 6:11-13 and 7:2-3. How is the enclosed paragraph (6:14–7:1) related to these?

3. Now study the outlines shown on Chart I, and compare them with the studies you have made already. Use this chart as a work sheet for recording observations already made and those that you will be making below in your analysis of each paragraph.

AN AMBASSADOR FOR CHRIST (5:20)   5:11—7:3

Chart I

AN AMBASSADOR'S MOTIVATIONS	AN AMBASSADOR'S MESSAGE	AN AMBASSADOR'S MARKS	AN AMBASSADOR'S FELLOWSHIP

5:11   5:16   5:21   6:1   6:11   "O, CORINTHIANS."   "Open your hearts"   6:14   "Come out from among them."   7:2   7:3   "Receive us"

MAINLY TESTIMONY AND DOCTRINE   MAINLY COMMAND AND EXHORTATION

HARDSHIPS (6:4-5)

CHRISTLIKE TRAITS (6:6-7)

DUAL EXPERIENCES (6:8-10)

B. Paragraph Analysis

1. *Paragraph 5:11-15*: An Ambassador's Motivations
The phrase "constraineth us" (v. 14) very clearly speaks of motivation. Analyze carefully each verse in the paragraph and determine what it was that motivated Paul to serve in God's vineyard. Record these:
verse 11

verse 12

verse 13

verses 14-15

Compare "terror of the Lord" (v. 11) and "love of Christ" (v. 14).

(See *Notes* on the former phrase.) Could it be that these phrases mean, respectively, our fear of the Lord and Christ's love to us?

What does Paul mean by verse 13?

In the first part of the verse, is he possibly referring to some accusation about him?

What important doctrines are taught in this paragraph?

2. *Paragraph 5:16-21*: An Ambassador's Message
It is in this paragraph that the word "ambassador" appears. The root of the Greek word means "elder." Read the following verses

where the word (or similar words) appears: Ephesians 6:20; Luke 14:32; 19:14 ("message"). What is an ambassador in everyday life?

_____

_____

What three parties are involved in any situation where an ambassador serves?

_____

_____

Study 5:20 in this connection. Who is an ambassador for Christ today?

_____

What strong word is repeated in verses 18-20, having to do with the message of Christ's ambassadors?

_____

What is meant by reconciliation?

_____

Who is reconciled to whom?

_____

What is restored in the reconciliation?

_____

Why do you think Paul wrote the last part of 5:20 if his readers were already Christians?

_____

_____

What is the condition of reconciliation, and what is the way? Answer this in the light of the following:
    (a) God "reconciled . . . by Jesus Christ" (5:18)
    (b) God "was in Christ" (5:19)
    (c) God "made him to be . . ." (5:21)
Compare the great truths taught in verses 17 and 21:

Verse	CHRIST	MAN
17		
21		

List the various truths of this paragraph that were the basic doctrines of Paul's message of salvation.

_____

_____

3. *Paragraph 6:1-10*: An Ambassador's Marks
Paul singles out three marks of an ambassador of Christ in these verses. Record them:
vv. 1-2 (Note: Render "in vain" as "without using it,"[3] and relate this to the phrase "workers together with him [God]"):

_____

v. 3:

_____

v. 4ff.:

_____

What are the two main subjects of verse 2?

_____

How does the subject of salvation (v. 2) apply to Christian workers already saved (v. 1)?

_____

Make a close study of the marks of Paul's ministry, as listed in verses 4-10. List these on Chart I under these headings: *Hardships* (6:4-5), *Christlike Traits* (6:6-7), and *Dual Experiences* (6:8-10). Must a true ambassador of Christ experience the "blizzard of troubles"[4] listed by Paul in these verses?

_____

What are the various triumphant notes of this paragraph? Note the last phrase.

_____

_____

3. Berkeley Version.
4. So called by Chrysostom.

4. *Paragraph 6:11-13*: An Ambassador's Fellowship
Read these three verses in a modern paraphrase. What is the meaning of verse 12?

_____

_____

How does verse 13 answer to verse 11?

_____

_____

5. *Paragraph 6:14–7:1*: An Ambassador's Fellowship (cont.)
To whom is Paul directing these words, according to the first part of verse 14?

_____

In the previous paragraph Paul spoke of the Christian fellowship that he and the Corinthians shared. What does he say about fellowship in this paragraph?

_____

_____

What are the contrasts of verses 14-16?

_____

_____

Record them on Chart H.
What answer to Paul's questions does the apostle expect to hear?

_____

_____

What is taught about *relationship to God* in verses 16 and 18?

_____

_____

What is taught about *separation* in 6:17 and 7:1?

_____

_____

6. *Paragraph 7:2-3*: An Ambassador's Fellowship (cont.)
These two verses echo the warm sentiment of the earlier paragraph 6:11-13.[5] Think about what Paul was really saying in the

5. The Greek word translated "receive" in the KJV means "make room for." Compare Mark 2:2 where the same Greek word appears again as "receive."

words "Ye are in our hearts to die and live with you." Why was such a sentiment of significant especially at this time?

III. NOTES

1. *"Terror of the Lord"* (5:11). This is the Christian's godly fear of the Lord. As Morgan observes, it is not a fear that God will hurt me but a fear that I might grieve the Lord.[6]

2. *"We persuade men; but we are made manifest unto God"* (5:11). The order and emphasis of the Greek original is: "Men we are persuading; but to God we have been made manifest."[7]

3. *"The love of Christ constraineth us"* (5:14). The idea of the verb "constraineth" is "not urging or driving, but shutting up to one line and purpose, as in a narrow, walled road."[8] Compare Philippians 1:23 and Luke 12:50 ("strait," "straitened").

4. *"Yet now henceforth know we him no more"* (5:16). *Today's English Version* represents the last half of verse 16 thus: "Even if at one time we judged Christ according to human standards, we no longer do so." Of Paul's former opinion of Jesus, Tasker comments,

> Paul admits that in his pre-conversion days he had judged Jesus by external considerations in the light of the prejudices of his upbringing, and he had concluded that it was impossible that one born in such obscurity, living in such restricted circumstances and dying such a humiliating death could be the Christ that the Jews were expecting. Consequently he had dismissed Him and persecuted His followers.[9]

5. *"Ambassadors for Christ"* (5:20). The role of an ambassador in international polity has not changed much over the years. As you read the following description by Lightfoot, apply it to ambassadorship for Christ:

> The ambassador, before acting, receives a commission from the power for whom he acts. The ambassador, while acting, acts not only as an agent but as a representative of his sovereign. Last, the ambassador's duty is not merely to deliver a defi-

6. G. Campbell Morgan, *The Corinthian Letters of Paul*, p. 158.
7. Wick Broomall, "The Second Epistle to the Corinthians," p.. 1271.
8. Marvin R. Vincent, *Word Studies in the New Testament*, 3:320.
9. R. V. G. Tasker, *The Second Epistle of Paul to the Corinthians*, p. 87.

nite message, to carry out a definite policy, but he is obliged to watch for opportunities, to study characters, to cast about for expedients, so that he may place it before his hearers in its most attractive form. He is a diplomatist.[10]

6. *"Be ye reconciled to God"* (5:20). The whole verse reads as though Paul is appealing to his Corinthian readers, who are already saved, to be reconciled to God. Some see in this a call for a fresh experience of reconciliation, or, as Calvin would say, for daily remission of sins.[11] It should be observed that no Greek pronoun for "you" or "ye" appears in the verse. This would support the view that "at this point the Apostle is concerned with the ministry of reconciliation for the world at large rather than with its application to the special circumstances of the church in Corinth."[12] One paraphrase of the verse that uses the universal third-person pronoun instead of the specific second person, is Bruce's: "God, we may say, is extending His invitation to men through us as we urge them for Christ's sake to be reconciled to God."[13]

7. *"Workers together with him"* (6:1). Although the words "with him" are not in the original text, the context supports this. See also 1 Corinthians 3:9 for a similar reference.

8. *"Receive not the grace of God in vain"* (6:1). Paul's intention was something like this: Receive not the grace of God in an empty, hollow way, to no purpose. That is, let this grace really penetrate you, so that its power will work in you and out from you, and establish you in the face of tests and tribulations.

9. *"Belial"* (6:15). This Hebrew word means, by derivation, "worthlessness." Here it is another name for Satan. Refer to a Bible dictionary for a further explanation of the word.

IV. FOR THOUGHT AND DISCUSSION

1. What motivates you to be a living testimony of God's grace? Have you learned anything from Paul's example?

2. What do you consider to be important traits and functions of a Christian serving as an *ambassador* for Christ?

3. If you are studying in a group, discuss the various experiences, ways and virtues listed in Paul's testimony of 6:4-10. Does the fact that this is a true testimony of a *man* (not Jesus) say anything to you?

10. J. B. Lightfoot, as quoted by Alfred Plummer, *The Second Epistle of St. Paul to the Corinthians*, p. 185.
11. See Philip E. Hughes, *Paul's Second Epistle to the Corinthians*, p. 211.
12. Ibid.
13. F. F. Bruce, *The Letters of Paul, An Expanded Paraphrase*.

4. In what ways can Christians today sin by being "unequally yoked together with unbelievers" (6:14)?

5. Why is separation from worldliness (6:17–7:1) so important in Christian living?

V. FURTHER STUDY

Try to identify each phrase of Paul's testimony in 6:4-10 with some particular experience of his as recorded either in Acts or the epistles. See how many of these you can so identify. Outside sources like commentaries and a book on the life of Paul will help you do this research.

VI. WORDS TO PONDER

For God took the sinless Christ and poured into Him our sins. Then, in exchange, He poured God's goodness into us! (5:21, TLB).

Lesson 8

Corinthians 7:4-16

Joy in Tribulation

Paul concludes the first major division (1:3–7:16) of his epistle on the triumphant note of joy. The tone of the opening verses of the epistle was just as bright. Recall that the title of Lesson 3 was Comfort in Tribulation (1:3-11) and compare this with the title of this lesson, Joy in Tribulation. Observe especially that Paul found comfort and joy not only when the winds were favorable, but— more important—when they were adverse and severe. The practical aim of your study of this lesson will be to find out how the apostle could honestly say, without exaggeration, "I am exceeding joyful in all our tribulation" (7:4).

I. PREPARATION FOR ANALYSIS

1. Review your study of Lesson 3. Recall that two key words of 1:3-11 were "comfort" (same as "consolation") and "sufferings."
2. Review the section of Lesson 1 called "The Historical Setting of 2 Corinthians." Note especially the reference to the "painful" letter. What were the contents of that letter? Read 2 Corinthians 2:3-4 and compare its context (e.g., the occurrences of the word "sorry") with 7:8ff.

II. ANALYSIS

Segment to be analyzed: 7:4-16
Paragraph divisions: at verses 4, 8, 13b (at "yea")

A. General Analysis

1. Mark the paragraph divisions in your Bible. Then read the passage, underlining key repeated words and phrases as you read. Record these on Chart J.

63

Paul, Titus, and the Corinthians	4 exceeding joyful in all our tribulation
Paul and the Corinthians	8
Titus, Corinthians, and Paul	13b 16

2. What is the main subject of each paragraph? Try organizing on outline on Chart J. (This need not be specifically related to the title "Joy in Tribulation.")

3. Compare the opening and closing verses of the segment.

4. Observe every reference to *joy* in the segment. Record these below and identify the *cause* for rejoicing in each case.

VERSE	REJOICING	CAUSE of REJOICING

B. Paragraph Analysis

1. *Paragraph 7:4-7.*
How do verses 5 and 6 identify the various kinds of tribulations (v. 4) that Paul was experiencing?

_____

_____

Try to think of specific situations involving Paul that could have been the experiences he identifies here. (For example, what kind of "fears" may have been his at this time?) Compare "our flesh had no rest" (7:5) with "I had no rest in my spirit" (2:13).

_____

_____

What were the two things in which Paul found comfort from God (7:6-7)?

_____

_____

What does each of these phrases reveal about the Corinthians at this time?

(a) earnest desires:

_____

(b) mourning:

_____

(c) fervent mind:

_____

2. *Paragraph 7:8-13a.*
How often does the word "sorry" (and related words) appear in the paragraph?

_____

What originally brought on the sorrow spoken of here?

_____

_____

_____

Why could Paul rejoice over their sorrow (7:9)?

_____

What were the *fruits* of this sorrow, in the lives of the Corinthians ("what . . . it wrought," 7:11). List these below and identify what is good about each.

_____

_____

_____

_____

What two things are contrasted in verse 10?

_____

_____

Is Paul saying here that the Corinthians' sorrow eventually led to their salvation? Or is he citing a prime example of the fruits of godly sorrow, that of a kind of repentance that is associated with salvation?

_____

_____

3. *Paragraph 7:13b-16.*
What do you learn about Titus from these verses?

_____

What do you learn about the Corinthians?

What does verse 16 reveal about the relationship between Paul and the Corinthians at this time?

III. NOTES

1. *"Ye sorrowed to repentance"* (7:9). Repentance involves a change of view, a change of feeling, and a change of will. Paul says that the Corinthians' sorrow brought about a change of will ("ye sorrowed *to* repentance"), and for this Paul was happy. The phrase "I do not repent" (7:8) is better translated "I do not regret it." So also "not to be repented of" (7:10) should read "not to be regretted."

2. *"Godly sorrow"* (7:10). This phrase appears in different ways in modern versions. Examples are:

Berkeley: "the sorrow that God approves"
Moffatt: "the sorrow that God directs"
Bruce: "grief which comes from God"
TEV: "the sadness that is used by God"
NASB: "the sorrow that is according to the will of God"

3. *"Sorrow of the world"* (7:10). One writer describes this sorrow as "a compound of depression, sloth, and irritability which plunges a man into a lazy languor and works in him constant bitterness."[1] Tasker rightly observes, "All sorrow, whether it be due to disappointment, affliction, bereavement, or sin, is deadly in its operation so long as it remains unsanctified. In itself sorrow has no healing power. Godly sorrow . . . alone is remedial."[2]

IV. FOR THOUGHT AND DISCUSSION

1. What can be said for the person who takes a clear stand or action that is unpopular and unattractive at the time but is for the good in the long run? What can parents learn from this for the raising of their children?
2. What are different ways in which Christians can be used of God to comfort brethren who are overwhelmed by sorrow? Where is the fountainhead of all true comfort?

1. Francis Paget, quoted in Tasker, *The Second Epistle of Paul to the Corinthians*, p. 106.
2. Ibid.

3. Paul wrote, "We spake all things to you in truth" (7:14). Why is truth a foundation of successful Christian living?

4. List at least five important truths that you learned from this passage about Christian joy.

_____

_____

_____

_____

V. FURTHER STUDY

Study what the New Testament teaches about repentance. Among other things, what is the relation of repentance to faith in a person's salvation?

VI. SUMMARY OF 1:3–7:16

Now that you have finished studying the first major division of 2 Corinthians (1:3–7:16), it would be profitable to review its content before moving on to the next lesson. The following excerpt from Chart C represents the contents of the six segments. See how much of each segment you can recall with the aid of this outline.

1:3	1:12	2:14	4:7	5:11	7:4 7:16
CONSOLATION	RECONCILIATION	MINISTRATION	LIMITATION	ASSOCIATION	GRATIFICATION

All in all, the apostle wrote these things so that his forthcoming third visit to Corinth would be a success. The last verse of this division reveals that Paul was optimistic at this point. "How happy I am that I can depend on you completely!" (7:16, TEV). Paul is not saying that there are no more problems in the Corinthian church to be worked on. What he is suggesting is that now a good relationship with the Corinthians has been restored; he feels that his coming visit will be the occasion for the solution of the problems that remain and the completion of the tasks yet undone. These are the subjects of the remainder of the epistle, treated in the lessons that follow.

Lesson 9

Christian Giving

The epistle's second main division concerns a fund-raising project the Corinthians began a year earlier.[1] In his first letter Paul called this a "collection for the saints" (1 Cor. 16:1). Some Jewish Christians living in Jerusalem were poverty-stricken, and it was the apostle's conviction that financial help at this time would carry them through this critical experience. Paul was also wise enough to know that the spiritual benefits derived from the project by the donors would far outweigh the monetary worth of the gift itself. He saw here the implications of a *communion* of saints and a reminder of the greatness of divine grace. It is no wonder then that he devoted such a large amount of the epistle to the mundane subject of fund-raising.

This passage is the New Testament's classic treatise on Christian giving. The setting is far removed from all of us as to time, geography, and culture, but the principles involved bridge all those gaps. Make it your aim in this study to learn why, how, and when God wants you to give to the cause of His gospel.

I. PREPARATION FOR ANALYSIS

1. Read the other New Testament references to this collection for the saints at Jerusalem.
(a) *1 Corinthians 16:1-4* (before writing 2 Corinthians). Observe the orderly details of Paul's instructions. Note also the reference to the churches of Galatia. If the Corinthian church had followed

---

1. The interval of one year is cited in 8:10 and 8:2. It has been pointed out by some, however, that the Greek text translated "a year ago" should read "last year," which would make the interval something less than a year. (See R. V. G. Tasker, *The Second Epistle of Paul to the Corinthians*, p. 123.)

the instructions of verse 2, would the offering be ready when Paul arrived at the city?

(b) *Romans 15:25-27* (after writing 2 Corinthians). Romans was written from Corinth during Paul's three-month stay. Did the Corinthian church fulfill their pledge?

What does Paul teach here about mutual obligations and sharing among fellow believers?

(c) *Acts 24:17.* In Acts 21:15ff., Luke does not report anything about Paul's delivering the offering to the church at Jerusalem. Paul's testimony in Acts 24:17 may refer to this offering.

2. A question that is not answered by the New Testament passages is, What brought on this poverty situation at Jerusalem? Various explanations have been offered, including those mentioned below:

> Augustine suggests that the poverty at Jerusalem was the result of the community of goods (Acts 4:32) . . . without careful organization of labour. . . . But there were other causes. Jerusalem had a pauperized population, dependent on the periodical influx of visitors. The Jewish world, from Cicero's time at least, supported the poor of Jerusalem by occasional subventions. As the Christian Jews came to be regarded as a distinct body, they would lose their share in these doles; and the 'communism' of Acts 4:32 was but a temporary remedy. Most of the converts were, therefore, poor at the outset. They were probably 'boycotted' and otherwise persecuted by the unconverted Jews (1 Thess 2:14; James 2:6), and their position would be similar to that of Hindoo [sic] Christians excluded from their caste, or Protestants in the West of Ireland.[2]

Why do you think the New Testament is virtually silent on such backgrounds of this plight?

2. A. Robertson and A. Plummer, *First Epistle of St. Paul to the Corinthians*, p. 382.

3. Recall your study of last lesson. Has there been reconciliation and restoration of confidence? (cf. 7:16). One writer has observed that "after restoring friendly relations with persons who have been cherishing resentment against us, we do not think it politic to begin at once to ask favours or to remind them of their duties; and yet this is just what the Apostle feels bound to do with the Corinthians, to whom he has only just become reconciled."[3] Keep this in mind as you study the passage and observe how Paul undertakes such a bold "diplomatic" mission.

4. Recall what cities of Macedonia Paul evangelized on his second missionary journey (Acts 15:36–18:22). The "churches of Macedonia" (2 Cor. 8:1) were located in these cities.

5. Read acts 11:27-30 for an earlier instance of when Christians sent material aid to brethren in need. (Cf. Gal. 6:10).

6. Review Chart C for the context of this passage in the scope of the entire epistle. Note especially the outlines of *time* and *tone*, excerpted in Chart K.

CONTEXT OF 8:1—9:15   **Chart K**

		THIS LESSON			
1:3		8:1	9:15	10:1	13:10
PAST		PRESENT		FUTURE	
TONE	FORGIVENESS, RECONCILIATION, GRATITUDE	CONFIDENCE		VINDICATION	

II. ANALYSIS

Segment to be analyzed: 8:1–9:15
Paragraph divisions: at verses 8:1, 6, 10, 16; 9:1, 6, 12

A. General Analysis

1. Follow the procedures of previous lessons by first marking the paragraph divisions in your Bible and then reading the entire segment with these divisions in mind.

3. Alfred Plummer, *Second Epistle of St. Paul to the Corinthians*, p. 231.

2. Now determine the main point of each paragraph and record these in the oblique sections of Chart L.

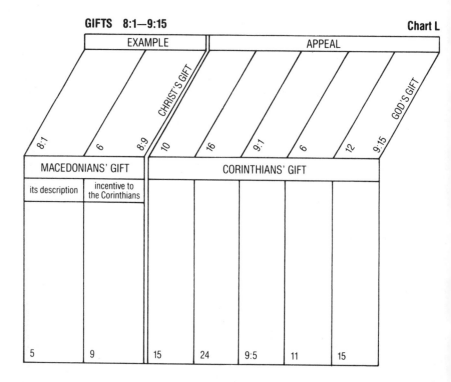

3. How does Chart L show this segment to be of two main parts? Scan the two chapters and try to justify this breakdown. Note that although Paul begins to write about the Corinthians' gift at 8:6 ("finish in *you*"), the division on the chart labeled Corinthians' Gift does not begin until 8:10. The reason for including paragraph 8:6-9 in the Macedonian section is that Paul's point in citing the example of the Macedonians is brought into focus in 8:6ff. (cf. "finish in you *the same grace also*," 8:6).

4. What is the climactic verse of each part? Mark these clearly in your Bible.

5. Does the word "money" appear in these two chapters? Consult an exhaustive concordance to see the distribution of this word in the New Testament.

6. Use Chart L as a work sheet for recording your studies as you move along in analysis.

B. Paragraph Analysis

1. *Paragraph 8:1-5:* Example of the Macedonians
Observe how the opening verse refers to the grace of God. How appropriate is this in view of what the entire segment is about?

_____

_____

What connection was there between God's grace bestowed on the churches (8:1) and their gift (8:2-5)?

_____

_____

What place did the Lord have in this Macedonian fund-raising project (8:5)?

_____

The translation "not as we hoped" (8:5) suggests a wrong meaning. A clearer reading is, "It was more than we could have hoped for!" (TEV). List all the truths taught in this paragraph about Christian giving.

_____

_____

_____

_____

2. *Paragraph 8:6-9:* Incentives for the Corinthians
How is the example of the Macedonians carried over into this paragraph?

_____

_____

What kind of incentive is the basis for Paul's solicitation in verse 7?

_____

_____

What are the example and incentive in verse 9?

_____

Compare verse 9 with verse 2. When was it that Christ "became poor"?

_____

_____

3. *Paragraph 8:10-15*: Appeal for Performance
What is taught in these verses about a *pledge* and the *performance* of it?

_____

_____

Why is a willing spirit so vital in Christian giving?

_____

What is a Christian's obligation as to how much money he should give to the work of the Lord?

_____

What does Paul teach in verses 13-15 about equalization?

_____

What kind of "abundance" (8:14) may the Jerusalem saints have had when Paul wrote this letter?

_____

In what sense were the Corinthians enjoying what had come from Jerusalem?

_____

4. *Paragraph 8:16-24*: Credentials of the Collectors
Note the references to the three collectors in verses 16, 18, and 22. Record what is said about each.
(a) Titus (8:16-17, 23):

_____

_____

(b) "the brother" (8:18-21, 23):

_____

_____

(c) "our brother" (8:23):

_____

_____

What lesson can be learned from this paragraph about how to administer fund-raising projects like this?

_____

_____

What is the important teaching of the last phrase of "honest . . . not only in the sight of the Lord, but also in the sight of men"?

_____

What does verse 24 teach about *works* in the Christian life?

_____

5. *Paragraph 9:1-5*: Mission of the Collectors
The main point of this paragraph centers around the two phrases: "I know" (9:2); "Yet have I sent" (9:3). In your own words, what is that main point?

_____

What does this paragraph reveal about Paul's understanding of human nature?

_____

Compare the two references to readiness:
    (a) "Achaia made preparations a year ago" (9:2)[4]
    (b) "that the same [gift] might be ready [now]" (9:5)
6. *Paragraph 9:6-11*: Generous Giving
In this paragraph Paul is still thinking about the collection for the poor but only as an illustration of Christian giving in its boundless, spiritual dimensions. The hand gift is a tangible expression of the heart gift. In these verses Paul writes especially about heart gifts. Make a list of the various teachings of this paragraph on Christian giving.

_____

_____

_____

How is God brought into this discussion of giving? (Note: The three verbs "minister," "multiply," and "increase" in verse 10 should be preceded by the word "will."[5])

_____

4. The KJV reads "was ready." Tasker says that the verb probably should be translated as "made preparations," similar to 1 Cor. 13:8 (p. 123).
5. This future-indicative form is supported by the most ancient manuscripts.

Note the repetition of "all" (and similar terms) in verse 8. How does this impress you?

---

7. *Paragraph 9:12-15*: Giving Begets Thanksgiving
What fruits of the Corinthians' gift are mentioned in these verses?

Read verses 13 and 14 in a modern paraphrase for a clearer rendering of the text. How does the subject of thanksgiving in these verses lead up to the grand finale of the section in verse 15?

What do you think Paul means by "unspeakable gift"?

Compare these different renderings of the concluding exclamation:[6]

(a) "God be thanked for His great gift—a gift no tongue can describe!" *(Expanded Paraphrase)*.

(b) "Let us thank God for his priceless gift!" (TEV).

(c) "Thanks be to God for His indescribable gift!" (NASB).

(d) "Thank God for His Son—His Gift too wonderful for words" (TLB).

III. NOTES

1. *"Grace"* (8:1). This word appears seven times in these two chapters of the King James Version. The same Greek word is translated "gift" in 8:4. In 8:19 the translation is "grace," though it is clear that the monetary *gift* is meant. The two words are in a sense interchangeable, since grace is an undeserved gift. It does not surprise us therefore to observe *grace* as a key word in a passage about a monetary gift.

2. *"Liberality"* (8:2). This is the same word that appears as "simplicity" in Romans 12:8: "He that giveth, let him do it with simplicity." This kind of giving is single-minded, uncalculating, free from ulterior motives. On the structure of 2 Corinthians 8:2,

---

6. Some expositors see in this phrase only a reference to God's grace bestowed on His people (cf. 8:1), bringing forth this generous contribution for the Jerusalem saints. (See Phillips's paraphrase of 9:15.)

Vincent suggests a reading that shows two parallel clauses: "How that in much proof of affliction was the abundance of their joy, and their deep poverty abounded unto the riches of their singleness."

3. *"Forwardness"* (8:8). The Greek word so translated has in it the ideas of eagerness, earnestness, and carefulness. The word appears throughout the King James Version in seven different ways: diligence, care, business, forwardness, earnest care, carefulness, haste.

4. *"We have sent"* (8:18). In effect, Paul meant "we are sending" (see TEV). This applies also to 9:3. When the Corinthians received the letter, the commissioning of the three emissaries was a past event. That is how Paul projected his thought as he wrote this.

5. *"The brother"* (8:18); *"our brother"* (8:22). We do not know the identity of these two brethren. Among the names suggested are: Trophimus, Luke, Gaius, Tychicus, Erastus, Aristarchus.

6. *"This abundance"* (8:20). This is the only appearance of the Greek word in the New Testament. The reference is to the *large size* of the contribution. It is understandable why most suspicions of financial programs of Christian organizations arise when extra-large amounts of money are involved. Read 8:20 with this in mind.

7. *"God loveth a cheerful giver"* (9:7). Paul may have had Proverbs 22:9 in mind when he wrote this. One translation of the Greek Septuagint version of the Proverbs passage is, "God blesseth a man who is cheerful and a giver." The order of the Greek words in the Corinthian passage in this: cheerful, for, giver, loves, God. Emphasis is on the first word, *cheerful.*[7]

8. *"Sufficiency"* (9:8). There is a twofold meaning in the word:[8] (a) self-sufficiency—the feeling of being able to rely on one's own resources without having to look to others; and (b) contentment—the satisfaction that comes of the self-sufficiency.

IV. FOR THOUGHT AND DISCUSSION

1. What lessons from this passage can be applied to fund-raising campaigns in Christian work?

2. What does the passage teach about
   (a) the amount of one's giving
   (b) rewards for giving

---

7. The Greek word so translated is *hilaron,* from which comes our word *hilarious.* (See also Rom. 12:8.)
8. See Tasker, pp. 126-27.

(c) making and fulfilling pledges to give
(d) attitudes in giving

3. How do you account for the Jerusalem saints' poverty in view of the "sufficiency" spoken about in 9:6-11?

4. What is the world's greatest need today? Can it be filled? What is the biggest gift you personally can give? Think about these lines:

> "Withhold not the Gospel from souls needing bread,
>   For giving is living," the bright angel said.
> "And must I be giving again and again?"
>   My peevish and pitiless answer ran.
> "On no, " said the angel, thus piercing me through,
> "Just give till the Saviour stops giving to you."
>
> (Anonymous)

V. FURTHER STUDY

The Bible is a story of grace. Study the word *grace* as it is used throughout Scripture: first, as an attribute of God, and second, as a way of living for God's people.

VI. WORDS TO PONDER

It is a joyful giver that God loveth (9:7).

An illustration: "Receiving a friend with a cheerful countenance and giving him nothing is better than giving him everything with a gloomy countenance" (paraphrase of a rabbinical saying).

Authority and Approval of a True Ministry

Paul devotes the remainder of his letter, beginning at 10:1, to vindicating his apostolic ministry. At one point in this section he states why such vindication is necessary: "Since ye seek a proof of Christ speaking in me" (13:3). Not all the Corinthians were guilty of such suspicion or antagonism. In fact, most of them were *with* Paul and were anxious to support his ministry in every way. (Read 7:16 again.) The instigators of opposition were men from without the Corinthian fellowship (cf. 11:4) who were trying to lure some of those Christians away from their loyalties. As long as there was this thorn in the group, Paul would do everything he could to remove it and the festering that it threatened.

The fact that four chapters (or 30 percent) of the entire epistle are devoted to this theme tells us that Paul did not think lightly of this problem at Corinth.[1] Besides this, we can understand the urgency of such an apologetic stand before the entire Christian world of the first century. A false gospel (11:4) as well as the true was being broadcast around the "world," and people were asking, "Who are the gospel's true ministers, and who are the false?" Paul's second letter to the Corinthians gave the answer not only to the church at Corinth but to people everywhere, of all time. As you study these four chapters, look especially for the credentials of a true witness for Christ in the work of the gospel.

I. PREPARATION FOR ANALYSIS

1. Chart M contains excerpts from the original survey Chart C. Observe the various comparisons made of the three main divisions of 2 Corinthians. Review your study of chapters 1-9 in the context of

---

1. Read the following passages that reveal something of the dark side of the Corinthian scene at this time: 11:3-4; 12:20-21; 13:5-7, 11.

this chart. Note the outline on "we" chapters and "I" chapters. Justify these identifications by scanning the first verse of each chapter in the epistle.[2]

CONTEXT OF 10:1—13:10   **Chart M**

1:3	8:1	10:1 13:10
TESTIMONIAL AND DIDACTIC	PRACTICAL	APOLOGETIC
the "we" chapters	"we" and "I"	the "I" chapters
SKETCH OF PAUL'S MINISTRY	A PROJECT OF PAUL'S MINISTRY	VINDICATION OF PAUL'S MINISTRY
Ephesus to Macedonia: change of itinerary explained	At Macedonia: preparation for the visit to Corinth	To Corinth: certainty and imminence of the visit

Why do you think Paul reserved the apologetic section for the last part of his letter?

_____

_____

2. In view of its subject matter, would you expect the tone of 10:1–13:10 to be any different from that of the preceding two sections? Read the first sentence of each paragraph of 10:1–13:10, observing the general atmosphere that prevails in this section.[3]

3. Refer to survey Chart C and observe the four verses out of the four segments of 10:1–13:10 that are related to 13:3.

4. Keep at least one contemporary translation of the New Testament at your side as you study the next four chapters of 2 Corin-

---

2. This study could be extended to the first verse of each paragraph, with the same results.

3. Destructive critics see this change of tone in the last four chapters as evidence that the chapters were not originally part of the epistle. But the tone changes because of the distinct purpose of these last four chapters. As Lenski comments, "The very restraint that is evident in the nine chapters shows that Paul reserved the demolition of the Judaizers for the final part of his letter" (R. C. H. Lenski, *The Interpretation of St. Paul's First and Second Epistles to the Corinthians*, p. 1194.)

thians. This will help you understand verses that are difficult either because they are ambiguous or awkward in structure.[4]
5. See the section *Further Study* concerning the *unity* of Paul's second epistle to the Corinthians.

II. ANALYSIS

Segment to be analyzed: 10:1-18
Paragraph divisions: at verses 1, 7, 12

A. General Analysis

1. Read the chapter once, underlining key words and phrases. Compare the text in a modern version.
2. What different things does Paul defend in this chapter? Observe how he brings the subject of God and Christ into the discussion.
3. Note the main topical study of Chart N titled Approved by the Lord. Locate in each paragraph the verse that is the basis for each of the three points: In Walk; In Consistency; In Glorying.
4. Observe on the chart the outline Weapons—Authority—Province of Labor. What phrases or verses in the text support these points? Record these on Chart N. Use the chart also to record other observations that you will be making in the remainder of this study.
5. Now focus your attention more minutely on each paragraph as a unit. In such analysis be conscious of *words, phrases*, and *sentences*. Study them individually and in their relation to each other.

B. Paragraph Analysis

1. *Paragraph 10:1-6*: The Weapons of Paul's Mission
First, make notations in your Bible on the following:
    (a) The meaning of the word "base" (10:1, KJV): see *Notes*.
    (b) Read "think to me" (v. 2) as "count on being" and "think of us" as "count us."
    (c) The parenthesis marks of verse 4 may be dropped.

---

4. The King James translation of this section of the epistle contains more than a few unclear readings. Vincent says of this, "Perhaps no portion of the New Testament furnishes a better illustration of the need of revision than the A.V. of this and the succeeding chapters" (Marvin R. Vincent, *Word Studies in the New Testament*, 3:344fn.).

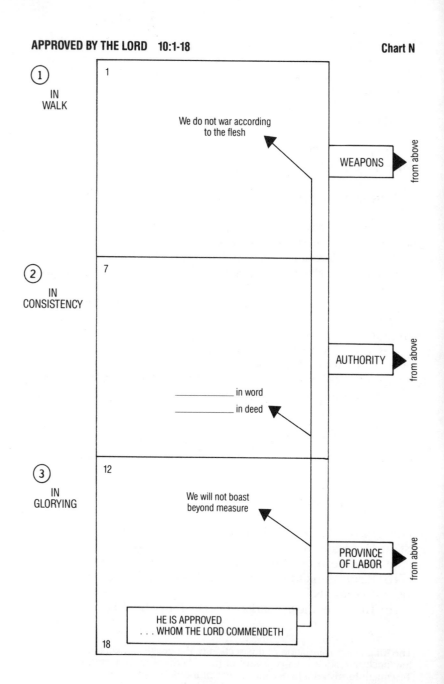

(1) IN WALK

1

We do not war according to the flesh

WEAPONS — from above

(2) IN CONSISTENCY

7

_____ in word
_____ in deed

AUTHORITY — from above

(3) IN GLORYING

12

We will not boast beyond measure

PROVINCE OF LABOR — from above

HE IS APPROVED
. . . WHOM THE LORD COMMENDETH

18

(d) Compare this rendering of verse 6: "We are prepared also to punish all disobedience, when your obedience is fully expressed" (Berkeley).
Compare verse 10 and verse 1, regarding Paul's presence and absence.
Observe the phrase "say they" in verse 10. Paul likely meant this in verse 1 also, paraphrased thus, "I who am said to be meek and mild when I am with you, but . . . ." (TEV). In view of this, what charge was leveled against Paul by his opponents, as represented by verse 1?

_____

What were Paul's two answers in verse 2?

_____

_____

What other charge was made against Paul, according to the last part of verse 2?

_____

How does Paul answer this in the verses that follow?

_____

_____

What does Paul plead for ("beseech") in verses 1 and 2?

_____

Why is there the repetition of "I beseech"?

_____

Relate the reference to Christ's "meekness and gentleness" to what Paul meant by "base" (10:1). Read verse 3. Distinguish between:
(a) "walk in the flesh"

_____

_____

(b) "war after the flesh"

_____

_____

How does Paul describe the weapons of his warfare in 10:4?

_____

_____

Note how verses 5 and 67 apply the metaphor of "pulling down of strong holds" (10:4). Paul cites three things he is able to do with his "mighty" weapons. Record the object of each:

	OBJECT
casting down	
bringing into captivity	
having a readiness to revenge	

Note the striking contrast between what some Corinthians were saying about Paul (10:1) and what he was actually accomplishing (10:3-6).

2. *Paragraph 10:7-11*: The Authority of Paul's Mission
What charges were made against Paul according to this paragraph?

_____

_____

What were Paul's answers?

_____

_____

What do these verses tell about Paul's

(a) relationship to Christ: _____

_____

(b) authority in ministering: _____

_____

(c) purposes in ministering: _____

_____

(d) consistency in ministering: _____

_____

3. *Paragraph 10:12-18*: The Extent of Paul's Mission
How is this paragraph about Paul's *preaching* a strong rebuttal to the charge of the previous paragraph that "his bodily presence [was] . . . weak, and his speech contemptible" (10:10)?

_____

_____

84

Observe the frequent occurrences of these words in the paragraph: *measure, rule, commend, boast, glory.* (Underline these words in your Bible.) What does this suggest about the main subject of the paragraph?

_____

Note also how often the word "but" appears. Be alert to the various contrasts in the paragraph that this small word introduces. Whom does Paul write about in verse 12?

_____

Who is the subject of the remaining verses?

_____

(Note: The phrase "he that commendeth himself" in the closing verse 18 refers back to what words in the opening verse 12?)

_____

Study carefully the subject of "measure." Whenever the word appears in the text, think of *standard, evaluation, measuring stick.* (Our English word *meter* comes from the Greek *metron*, translated "measure.") Answer the following:
(a) What was the measuring stick used by the false apostles (10:12)?

_____

_____

What was wrong with this?

_____

(b) What measuring stick ("rule") did Paul use to evaluate his ministry (10:13)?

_____

(c) Did the province of labor that was assigned to Paul include Corinth (10:13*b*)?[5] Did it include regions beyond Corinth (10:16)?

_____

Did it include places where other men had already witnessed (10:15-16)?

_____

---

5. The awkward reading of verse 14*a* is clarified in Bruce's *Expanded Paraphrase*: "I am not exceeding the terms of my commission as though you did not rightly fall within my province."

(d) What was an indicator to Paul that he should move further on with the gospel to new territories (10:15-16)?

(e) The last part of verse 14 is translated thus by the Berkeley Version: "For we were the first to reach you with the good news about Christ." How did such pioneering enhance Paul's credentials and answer the false apostles' charges?

(f) According to these verses, did Paul minister according to standards set up by God?

How are the subjects of glory (v. 17) and commendation (v. 18) related to the subject of God's standards?

How do the two verses conclude the discussion of the paragraph?

III. NOTES

1. *"Base among you"* (10:1). The word for "base" is sometimes translated meek, humble, or lowly. It is the opposite of "bold" (also v.1). Sometimes the word is used to represent a noble virtue (e.g., "lowly" in Matt. 11:29), but here the word is applied to Paul in a derogatory sense, such as "fainthearted" or "cowardly." Lenski comments about the false insinuations of this charge:

> Paul is such a lowly fellow, and he cannot face anyone with manly courage, he is courageous only when he is at a safe distance (v. 1). The answer to that is the tremendous campaign which he is directing as commander-in-chief by demolishing the mightiest enemy fortifications (v. 2-6). Timid, little cowards who make fists at a distance do not wreck fortresses![6]

6. Lenski, p. 224.

2. *"As if we walked according to the flesh"* (10:2). One translation is "acting in worldly fashion" *(Revised Standard Version)*.

3. *"When your obedience is fulfilled"* (10:6). Of this verse, Charles Hodge comments that Paul "would not resort to severity until all other means had failed, and until it had become fully manifest who among the Corinthians would submit to God, and who would persist in their disobedience."[7]

4. *"Somewhat more"* (10:8). That is, excessively.

5. *"Without our measure"* (10:13). The phrase means "beyond measure." The word "measure" suggests a determined extent and is so used also in Romans 12:3.

6. *"The regions beyond you"* (10:16). "The farther Paul penetrated the Gentile world with the gospel, the nearer he came to the mark and the measure that God had set for him."[8]

IV. FOR THOUGHT AND DISCUSSION

1. Evangelization keeps advancing into enemy territory, the realm of spiritual darkness, unbelief. What weapons does a soldier of Christ have at his disposal? As to *methods* of Christian service, are there standards of practice, or does anything "go"?

2. What has been your experience in this: "bringing into captivity every thought to the obedience of Christ" (10:5)? In what ways is this discipline manifested in one's everyday living?

3. What is the primary purpose of the church's ministry: edification or destruction? (Cf. 10:8.)

4. What is the difference between proselytism and evangelism? Lenski observes that proselyters today "make it their business and their delight to invade the congregations which were long ago built up in the true gospel. The devil could not remain in hell, he had to break into Eden (11:3)"[9]

5. What have you learned in this lesson about:
(a) Consistency in Christian living
(b) Glorying that is acceptable to God
(c) Commendation by the Lord

V. FURTHER STUDY

1. Word studies are recommended for these words: meekness, gentleness, approved. Some of the verses to be consulted on

---

7. Charles Hodge, *Commentary on the Second Epistle to the Corinthians*, p. 237.
8. Lenski, p. 1227.
9. Ibid.

the last-named word are: Romans 3:5; 5:8; 16:1; 2 Corinthians 4:2; 6:4; 10:18; 12:11.

2. Consult outside sources for a discussion of the *unity* of this Corinthian epistle.[10] Here is one example of evidence supporting such a unity: "All of the hints found in the first seven chapters in regard to opposition and opponents in Corinth leave us at sea until the last four chapters bring the complete answer to the questions raised by those hints."[11]

VI. WORDS TO PONDER

A man is really approved when the Lord thinks well of him, not when he thinks well of himself (10:18, TEV).

10. For example, Lemski, pp. 1191-95.
11. Ibid., p. 1191.

Lesson 11

True and False Apostles

Paul has more to say in this epistle about his ministry and the charges of false religionists opposing him. We have seen in the previous lesson how the last two verses of chapter 10 conclude the message of the chapter. It may be noted here that the same two verses introduce the two subjects to be expanded in the passages of this lesson and the one that follows. These two subjects are *glory* (read 10:17) and *approval* (read 10:18). The passages dealing with them are:

> 11:1-15 True and False Apostles—*Approval* (Lesson 11)
> 11:16–12:13 What Paul Gloried In—*Glory* (Lesson 12)

It is from passages like these that we learn that although the opposition partly against Paul was a small minority in the Corinthian church, it was a formidable one. Paul was wise enough to know that evil begets evil—quickly, thoroughly, and destructively. So he spared no words in this part of his letter to expose the false apostles and reassure the faithful Corinthians of his own divinely approved credentials. As we have noted before, *Paul wanted his forthcoming visit to be a success.*

I. PREPARATION FOR ANALYSIS

1. On Paul's relationship to the spiritual experience of the Christians at Corinth, read 1 Corinthians 4:15; 9:1. Compare this with the picture of betrothal ("espoused") in 2 Corinthians 11:2*a*. Read a description of betrothal[1] in *Unger's Bible Dictionary*, page 698. Also read Ephesians 5:25-27 as background for the last metaphor of 2 Corinthians 11:2 ("present . . . as a chaste virgin").

---

1. Betrothal in Bible times had some (not many) resemblances to present-day engagements.

2. Read 1 Corinthians 9:4-15 concerning Paul's independence of the Corinthian church as far as financial support was involved. Compare Philippians 4:10, 15, where Paul writes about aid that he received from the church at Philippi.

3. "To visualize is to empathize." Put yourself in Paul's position, awaiting the journey to Corinth. Try to feel what Paul was feeling.

II. ANALYSIS

Segment to be analyzed: 11:1-15
Paragraph divisions: at verses 1, 7, 13

A. General Analysis

1. Use the following renderings in place of the King James Version text cited:

v. 4: "ye might well bear with him"—"you put up with it quite easily" (Berkeley)

v. 6: "be rude"—"am amateur" (TEV); "am unskilled" (RSV)

v. 6: "We have been throughly made manifest among you in all things."—We have in every way made perfectly clear to all of you" (Berkeley).

v. 7: "freely"—"without accepting any pay" (Williams)

v. 12: compare this entire verse in the King James Version with this rendering: "And what I do I will continue to do, in order to undermine the claim of those who would like to claim that in their boasted mission they work on the same terms as we do" (RSV).

2. Read the segment once to determine the main subject of each paragraph. Record these:

11:1-6

_____

11:7-12

_____

11:13-15

_____

3. Read the segment again, observing what parts of each paragraph are about Paul and what parts are about the false apostles. Compare your findings with those of Chart O.

4. Use Chart O as a work sheet to record observations made as you study the passage paragraph by paragraph.

PAUL	**1**	PREACHING
FALSE APOSTLES	**3** another Jesus / another spirit / another gospel [Serpent]	PREACHING
PAUL	**5**	PREACHING
PAUL	**7**	FINANCIAL SUPPORT
FALSE APOSTLES	**12**	FINANCIAL SUPPORT
FALSE APOSTLES	**13** TRANSFORMED INTO → apostles of Christ / angel of light / ministers of righteousness [Satan] **15**	FRAUD

91

B. Paragraph Analysis

1. *Paragraph 11:1-6:* Preaching
What do you learn about Paul from the first two verses?

_____

What is meant by "godly jealousy"?

_____

What spiritual truths are represented by the metaphors:
one husband

_____

chaste virgin

_____

What do you learn about the false apostles from verses 3-4?

_____

_____

What do you think Paul means by "the simplicity that is in Christ" (11:3)?

_____

_____

Is it possible that the false apostles were sponsoring a sophisticated intellectualism, similar to the heresy at Colossae? (Read Col. 2:8.)[2] To what was Paul referring by the phrases:
"another Jesus"

_____

"another spirit"

_____

"another gospel"

_____

Compare Galatians 1:6-10; 2:4 for a similar situation. What is the purpose of Paul's claims in verses 5-6?

_____

_____

To whom was he applying the words "the very chiefest apostles"?

_____

2. Colossians 1:8-23 also makes references to a Judaistic legalism that had crept into the church at Colossae. See *Notes* on 11:4.

2. *Paragraph 11:7-12*: Financial Support

When Paul had ministered at Corinth on his evangelistic mission there, he earned his living as a tentmaker, working for Aquila and Priscilla (Acts 18:1-4). The false apostles who moved in after he left apparently received pay for their "services" to the Christian group. Paul believed in wages for Christian service; in fact, he wrote at length in his first epistle defending wages (1 Cor. 9:3-14). But his opponents were charging that Paul had evil motives in not accepting pay for his services; hence his defense at this point in the epistle. Compare the first phrase of verse 7 with 1 Corinthians 9:3*a*. What reasons does Paul give for not wanting financial support from the Corinthians?

verse 7:

_____

verse 8:

_____

verse 9:

_____

verse 11:

_____

verse 12:

_____

3. *Paragraph 11:13-15*: Fraud

How does Paul identify his opponents (v. 13*a*)?

_____

Whose ministers are they really (vv. 14-15)?

_____

How do they *appear* to people (vv. 13-15)?

_____

What is their ultimate destiny (v. 15*b*)? Compare Philippians 3:18-19.

_____

NOTES

1. *"Simplicity"* (11:3). The same word is translated "single-ness" in Ephesians 6:5 and Colossians 3:22. The word also has the connotation of sincerity, unaffectedness.

2. *"Another gospel"* (11:4). "Although not so clearly as in Galatians, Paul seems to be referring to Judaizers, Christians who insisted upon circumcision and all the burdens it involved."[3]

3. *"The very chiefest apostles"* (11:5). Most of the older commentators[4] understood this to refer to the true apostolic circle (cf. "pillars," Gal. 2:9). It is now generally viewed as an ironical reference (e.g., "those super-apostles"), continuing the tone of irony in the last phrase of verse 4, "You seem so gullible: you believe whatever anyone tells you. . . . You swallow it all" (TLB).[5]

4. *"They may be found even as we"* (11:12). Various interpretations have been made of this verse. Morgan sees Paul as wishing his opponents also had to work for their living so that they also would be "found even as" Paul, not dependent on the Corinthians for their support.[6]

5. *"Satan . . . into an angel of light"* (11:14). An angel of light, appearing in the spiritual world of darkness, does not look like an *adversary*, which the word *Satan* literally means.

6. Satan's *"ministers . . . as the ministers of righteousness"* (11:15). "Satan does not come to us as Satan; neither does sin present itself as sin, but in the guise of virtue; and the teachers of error set themselves forth as the special advocates of truth."[7]

IV. FOR THOUGHT AND DISCUSSION

What have you learned from this passage about the following:

1. The responsibility of a Christian to nurture and guard a soul whom he has led to Christ

2. The deceitful methods of Satan to lure saints from the paths of righteousness

3. A Christian's need for discernment as he hears and reads what false teachers are presenting as the gospel of Jesus

4. How to deal with false teaching that contradicts the true gospel of the Bible

5. Why it is important to keep the financial aspect of Christian work above reproach

V. FURTHER STUDY

1. The church is now in the position of espousal (cf. 2 Cor. 11:2). Ultimately there will be the marriage of Christ and the bride

---

3. Berkeley Version, p. 201fn.
4. See G. Campbell Morgan, *The Corinthian Letters of Paul*, p. 172.
5. See R. V. G. Tasker, *The Second Epistle of Paul to the Corinthians*, pp. 148-49.
6. Morgan, p. 173.
7. Charles Hodge, *Commentary of the Second Epistle to the Corinthians*, p. 265.

(Church). Inquire into the New Testament teaching of this event. Key passages are Revelation 18:6-10 and Ephesians 5:27. (Cf. also John 3:29; Rev. 21:2, 9.)

2. Study what the Bible teaches about Satan. Sources to read are a book on doctrine, a Bible encyclopedia or dictionary, word studies, and a concordance.

VI. WORDS TO PONDER

Satan can change himself into an angel of light, so it is no wonder his servants can do it too, and seem like godly ministers (11:14-15a, TLB).

Lesson 12

2 Corinthians 11:16–12:13

Credentials of a True Ministry

In answer to the false apostles in Corinth, Paul presents a positive testimony of his credentials. In our last lesson we studied about the false apostles in Corinth who were preaching "another gospel" and discrediting Paul's apostleship. The passage of this lesson is Paul's positive testimony of credentials as a true minister of Christ. In earlier portions of the epistle he has compared himself with the false apostles but not as thoroughly and specifically as he does in this passage.[1] The subject has been building up to this climax, and Paul now feels compelled to submit a lengthy document of self-authentication (cf. 12:11). His motives in doing so remain selfless and constructive:

> It is for the Corinthians' sake that he is now going to match boldness with boldness, so that, acknowledging afresh what they have been tempted to forget, namely that HE IS THEIR TRUE GOSPELLER, they may reject the false apostles and their teachings and abide in the pure Christian truth in which they had been so earnestly instructed by him. . . .[2]

I. PREPARATION FOR ANALYSIS

You may want to do some biographical background reading as preparation for your study of this passage. Such reading includes:

1. The Acts account of Paul's life from the time of his conversion to the writing of 2 Corinthians: Acts 9:1–20:2. Note especially how the Lord foretold the experiences of suffering that Paul would have, as recorded in Acts 9:16.

---

1. Actually, the present passage is made up more of forthright *claim* than it is of *comparison.*
2. Philip E. Hughes, *Paul's Second Epistle to the Corinthians*, pp. 402-3, emphasis supplied.

2. Two testimonies of Paul in the book of Acts: 22:3-21; 26:2-23.

3. Biography of the life of Paul,[3] which incorporates information from Paul's epistles as well as from Acts.

4. Second Corinthians 6:4-10. Review your study of this paragraph in Lesson 7.

II. ANALYSIS

Segment to be analyzed: 11:16–12:13
Paragraph divisions: at verses 11:16, 21*b*, 20; 12:1, 7, 11 (mark these in your Bible)

A. General Analysis

1. Scan the segment once for general impressions. What is the *type* of content here (e.g., doctrine, testimony, exhortation)? Now read the passage a little more slowly, underlining key words and phrases in your Bible.
2. What subject is common to the opening verses of all the paragraphs?

_____

Try to identify what one main point Paul is trying to establish in each paragraph. Compare your conclusions with the outlines shown on Chart P.
3. Use Chart P as a work sheet to record observations as you continue to analyze each paragraph.
4. How is the first paragraph an introduction to the segment?

_____

_____

5. Note every reference to Paul's glorying in the segment.[4] Record your findings on Chart P.

B. Paragraph Analysis

1. *Introduction*: 11:16-21*a*
Compare 11:16 and 11:1 (e.g., "bear with me," and "receive me").

---

3. A recommended brief treatment is James Stalker, *The Life of St. Paul* (Westwood, N. J.: Revell, 1912).
4. The words "boast" (e.g., 11:16) and "glory" (as used by Paul in this passage) translate the same Greek word.

CREDENTIALS OF A TRUE MINISTRY (—12:12a) 11:16—12:13

EXPERIENCE

INTRODUCTION	TRIBULATION	HUMILIATION	VISION	AFFLICTION	COMPETITION
11:16	shipwreck 11:21b	basket 11:30 / 11:33	third heaven 12:1	thorn 12:7	wonders 12:11 / 12:13
The Experience	endurance	escape	exhilaration	sustenance	wonders
The Victory					PAUL'S GLORYING

What do you think Paul means by "I speak it not after the Lord"?

_____

_____

Compare verse 21 in a modern version. How does Paul justify his glorying in verses 19-21?

_____

_____

2. *Shipwreck*: 11:21*b*-29
What does Paul establish in verse 22?

_____

_____

Examine the long list of trials in 11:23ff. Look for any possible grouping. How does verse 28 strike you in the context of this paragraph?

_____

_____

3. *Basket*: 11:30-33[5]
What is the main point of each verse:
verse 30:

_____

verse 31:

_____

verse 32:

_____

verse 33:

_____

Why do you think Paul made a point of his escape by *basket*? Compare the basket experience with 11:30 and with the experience described in 12:1-6.[6]

_____

_____

5. The Berkeley Version makes the new paragraph begin with v. 18. Other versions prefer not to make a new paragraph division at all, since the opposition to Paul in v. 32 is similar to the examples cited earlier (e.g., v. 26).
6. Cf. Acts 9:23-25. For an extended discussion of the mention of Aretas in 2 Cor. 11:32, see Hughes, pp. 424-28.

4. *Third heaven*: 12:1-6
Most commentators see this as an experience of Paul himself. How does verse 5 support this view?

_____

If this was an experience of Paul, why would he not say so openly and clearly? What other aspects of the experience does Paul keep hidden?

_____

_____

How did the experience impress Paul? Why does he recall it at this point in the epistle (12:5-6)?

_____

_____

5. *Thorn*: 12:7-10
How was the thorn experience related to the visions of the previous paragraph?

_____

_____

What is meant by these expressions:
"thorn in the flesh"

_____

"messenger of Satan"

_____

What choice statement appears in this paragraph?

_____

Compare "my grace" and "my strength" (12:9).

_____

_____

What did Paul learn from this experience?

_____

_____

How is verse 10 a conclusion to all that precedes it in the segment?

_____

_____

6. *Wonders*: 12:11-13
What is the key statement of the paragraph?

How does the paragraph serve as a conclusion for the entire segment?

Compare 12:12 and 11:21.

III. NOTES

1. *"As a fool"* (11:16). In 11:1 Paul spoke of his apologetic as "folly." C. F. Kling comments, "This commendation of himself... he ironically calls a 'folly,' because it seemed to give undue importance to that which was insignificant and connected only with outward appearances."[7]

2. *"I speak it not after the Lord"* (11:17). This is not a denial of the divine inspiration of Paul's words. What Paul means is that he is not following any example of Christ in this, because Christ never spoke boastful words such as the Corinthians are forcing Paul to do (cf. 12:11).

3. Verses 20 and 21a. The *New English Bible* has this lively translation:

> If a man tyrannizes over you, exploits you, gets you in his clutches, puts on airs, and hits you in the face, you put up with it. And we, you say, have been weak! I admit the reproach.

4. *"Are they Israelites? So am I"* (11:22). "To Paul it was something thrilling to be in the midstream of God's age-old purposes for the whole of mankind through the chosen people of Israel."[8] Compare Philippians 3:4-6.

5. *"Through a window in a basket was I let down"* (11:33). The symbolism of condescension and dependency is reiterated by this triple description. It is as though Paul was saying, "Such unhe-

7. Lange's *Commentary on the Holy Scriptures, Corinthians*, p. 177.
8. Hughes, p. 403.

roic incidents have marked my course; I have been treated like a bale of goods in the course of labour for my King."[9]

6. *"I knew a man in Christ"* (12:2). Paul is speaking of himself here (cf. v. 5). The awesomeness of the experience is reflected in his not wanting to name himself.

7. *"Fourteen years ago"* (12:2).[10] This experience took place some time between Paul's conversion and his first missionary journey. (See *Further Study.*)

8. *"Third heaven"* (12:2). This is a reference to God's dwelling place in heaven, also called paradise in 12:4 (cf. Luke 23:43; Rev. 2:7). In Hebrew thought the first heaven was the atmosphere in which the birds fly; the second heaven, the region of sun, moon, and stars; and the third heaven, where God dwells.[11]

9. *"Thorn in the flesh"* (12:7). Taken semiliterally, this may refer to some physical malady or infirmity. (An eye disease, malaria, and epilepsy are possible afflictions suggested by commentators). Tasker favors the view that the thorn was *spiritual* in character, "sent by God 'for the flesh,' i.e., to prick the bubble of the apostle's arrogance, traces of which almost certainly lingered on even after he had been converted from Pharisaism."[12]

IV. FOR THOUGHT AND DISCUSSION

What different truths about affliction and persecution are taught by this passage? Apply these to your own life.

V. FURTHER STUDY

1. Where do you think Paul was when he had the vision of 12:2-6? For how long had he been a Christian? In answering these questions, consider the phrase "fourteen years ago" (12:2) in connection with this chronology:

A.D. 33—Saul's conversion
A.D. 36—To Tarsus (Acts 9:30)
A.D. c.43—To Antioch (Acts 11:25-26)
A.D. 47—First missionary journey launched (Acts 13:1ff.)
A.D. 56-57—2 Corinthians written

---

9. See A. W. Handley Moule, *The Second Epistle to the Corinthians*, p. 111. Also, note the last two words of 11:33 in the *The Living Bible* paraphrase .
10. The word "above" (v. 2) has no strong textual support, hence is omitted in most versions.
11. See W. C. G. Proctor, "II Corinthians: Commentary," in *The New Bible Commentary*, p. 999.
12. R. V. G. Tasker, *The Second Epistle of Paul to the Corinthians*, p. 175.

2. Consult various commentaries for a discussion of Paul's "thorn in the flesh."

VI. WORDS TO PONDER

My grace is all that you need: my power is most fully displayed when my people are weak (12:9, Bruce's *Expanded Paraphrase*).

Lesson 13

2 Corinthians 12:14–13:14

"Prepare for My Visit"

Our concluding study is about Paul's last words to the Christians at Corinth before his final visit. The apostle was concerned that this visit be a success. This, in fact, was the reason for his delay in going to them. He wanted them to clear up their own spiritual problems before he got there. In these last paragraphs of his letter his main burden was this: "Prepare for my visit, for I am ready to come to you."

I. PREPARATION FOR STUDY

1. Review the historical setting of 2 Corinthians that was discussed in Lesson 1. When did Paul's two visits to Corinth take place? Compare the phrase "the third time" in 12:14 and 13:1.

2. Review the highlights of 2 Corinthians up to this point. Since this final passage serves as a summary as well as a conclusion for the letter, it is helpful to recall what has been written before.

II. ANALYSIS

Segments to be analyzed: 12:14–13:10; and 13:11-14
Paragraph divisions: at verses 12:14, 19; 13:1, 5, 11, 14

1. Read the entire passage and note every reference to Paul's forthcoming visit (e.g., "I am coming to you," 13:1).
2. In what ways does the passage conclude the epistle?

104

3. Observe things Paul writes here that he had mentioned earlier in the epistle.[1] Record these.

_____

_____

_____

_____

4. Note any new subjects that he brings up.

_____

_____

_____

5. List any doctrinal teachings.

_____

_____

_____

6. What do you learn about the Corinthians here?

_____

_____

7. What do you learn about Paul here?

_____

_____

8. List the various truths taught by the concluding segment, 13:11-14. Relate these to the burden of the epistle.

_____

_____

_____

1. For example, compare 13:10 and 10:8.

III. NOTES

1. *"Being crafty"* (12:16). Paul is citing here what some Corinthians were saying about him: "But, someone will say, I was tricky and trapped you with lies" (TEV).
2. *"Reprobates"* (13:6). The Greek word means "disapproved on trial" (cf. "approved" of 13:7).
3. *"Farewell"* (13:11). Some translations read "rejoice," based partly on how the word was used in the first century. For example, it was a greeting at both meeting *and* parting.

IV. FOR THOUGHT AND DISCUSSION

Think again about the various aspects of Paul's ministry for Christ. What does this passage teach about the following:
  (a) the drive behind Paul's ministry (e.g., 12:14)
  (b) the aims of his ministry (12:19; 13:9)
  (c) the strength of his ministry (13:4)
  (d) the message of his ministry (e.g., 13:5)
  (e) the character of his ministry (13:8)

V. A SUMMARY EXERCISE FOR 2 CORINTHIANS

If you are studying in a group, let each member share with the others what he has learned in his study of 2 Corinthians. This may involve favorite verses, practical advice, important doctrines, or even small details that for some reason keep lingering in the memory.

VI. THE CLOSING BENEDICTION

The grace of our Lord, Jesus, Messiah,
    of Him whom we have preached to you,
And the love of our God,
    His sublime affection for you His children in His Son,
    made real to your hearts,
And the participation of the Holy Spirit,
    a full share to each of you, and a common and
    mutual enjoyment by all of you, of His indwelling
    and His power,
Be with all of you (13:14).[2]

---

2. Amplified phrases by H. W. Handley Moule, *The Second Epistle to the Corinthians*, p. 126.

Bibliography

COMMENTARIES AND TOPICAL STUDIES

Broomall, Wick. "The Second Epistle to the Corinthians." In *The Wycliffe Bible Commentary*, ed. Charles F. Pfeiffer and Everett F. Harrison. Chicago: Moody, 1962.

Hodge, Charles. *Commentary on the Second Epistle to the Corinthians*. Grand Rapids: Eerdmans, 1950.

Hughes, Philip E. *Paul's Second Epistle to the Corinthians*. The New International Commentary on the New Testament. Grand Rapids: Eerdmans, 1962.

Kling, C. F. *Lange's Commentary on the Holy Scriptures, Corinthians*. Reprint ed. Grand Rapids: Zondervan, n.d.

Luck, G. Coleman. *Second Corinthians*. Everyman's Bible Commentary. Chicago: Moody, 1959.

Morgan, G. Campbell. *The Corinthian Letters of Paul*. London: Oliphants, 1947.

Proctor, W. C. G. "II Corinthians: Commentary." In *The New Bible Commentary*, ed. F. Davidson, A. M. Stibbs, and E. F. Kevan. Grand Rapids: Eerdmans, 1953.

Scroggie, W. Graham. *Know Your Bible*. Vol. 2. London: Pickering & Inglis, n.d.

RESOURCES FOR FURTHER STUDY

Modern Versions

Bruce, F. F. *The Letters of Paul, An Expanded Paraphrase*. Grand Rapids: Eerdmans, 1965.

Everyday Bible. New Testament Study Edition. Minneapolis: World Wide, 1988.

Good News for Modern Man. Today's English Version. New York: American Bible Society, 1966.

New American Standard Bible. Chicago: Moody, 1973.

New Berkeley Version. Rev. ed. Grand Rapids: Zondervan, 1969.

New English Bible. New Testament. Oxford: U. Press, 1961.

New International Version Study Bible. Grand Rapids: Zondervan, 1985.

Phillips, J. B. *Letters to Young Churches.* New York: Thomas Nelson & Sons, 1946.

Other Helps

Jensen, Irving L. *Jensen's Survey of the New Testament.* Chicago: Moody, 1981.

Nave, J. Orville. *Nave's Topical Bible.* Chicago: Moody, n.d. This treats topics of the Bible, which differentiates it from a concordance (words).

Strong, James. *The Exhaustive Concordance of the Bible.* New York: Abingdon, 1890.

Unger, Merrill F. *New Unger's Bible Dictionary.* Chicago: Moody, 1988.

Vincent, Marvin R. *Word Studies in the New Testament.* Vol. 3. Grand Rapids: Eerdmans, 1946. More like a commentary on key words and phrases of the Bible text.

Vine, W. E. *An Expository Dictionary of New Testament Words.* Westwood, N.J.: Revell, 1961. Excellent source book for word studies.

Young, Robert. *Analytical Concordance to the Bible.* Grand Rapids: Eerdmans, n.d.